true green home

Beleura Hill House by Graham Jones Design. Photo: Warren Kirby

# true green home

## 100 ideas to help you create a greener home

Kim McKay and Jenny Bonnin

ABC Books

Published by ABC Books for the
AUSTRALIAN BROADCASTING CORPORATION
GPO Box 9994 Sydney NSW 2001

Copyright © True Green (Global) Pty Ltd 2008

*First published October 2008*

All rights reserved. No part of this publication may be reproduced, stored in a retrieval system or transmitted in any form or by any means, electronic, mechanical, photocopying, recording or otherwise, without the prior written permission of the Australian Broadcasting Corporation.

ISBN 978 0 7333 2287 7

*Design and image selection by Marian Kyte*
*Research and editing by Viviane Stappmanns*
*Colour reproduction by Graphic Print Group, Adelaide*
*Printed in Hong Kong by Quality Printing*

5 4 3 2 1

A percentage of proceeds from the sale of *True Green Home* benefits Clean Up Australia.

*True Green Home* has purchased carbon offsets to neutralise emissions produced by the printing of this book.

True Green is a registered trademark of True Green (Global) Pty Ltd.

Cover photo: Corbis Australia.

The paper used to print this book is made from wood grown in sustainable forests.

The ABC is not responsible for the content found on non-ABC internet sites referred to in this book.

The internet, your local council, federal and state governments all produce terrific information and advice on how to live a greener life, with online journals, magazines and websites dedicated to a greener world. We gratefully acknowledge the valuable resources in the research of *True Green Home* and encourage you to explore the many sites listed on pages 132–135 for even more information and inspiration to create a better and cleaner world.

# contents

**case studies**

- 22 brisbane sustainable house
- 34 caroline pidcock
- 46 luke middleton
- 58 kirsty máté
- 70 jeremy davies
- 82 ewan mceoin
- 94 pierce cody
- 106 sustainable gardening australia
- 118 michael mobbs
- 130 frank fisher

| | |
|---|---|
| foreword | 7 |
| introduction | 8 |
| **home green home** | 11 |
| **green energy** | 23 |
| **green living** | 35 |
| **eco-kitchen** | 47 |
| **bathroom basics** | 59 |
| **sleeping green** | 71 |
| **DIY green rooms** | 83 |
| **green housekeeping** | 95 |
| **a greener garden** | 107 |
| **around the house** | 119 |
| resources | 131 |
| acknowledgements | 143 |

Westham Farmhouse won the 2007 Energy Australia National Trust Award for the best historic renovation under $1 million and Ian Kiernan was awarded the National Trust Lifetime Achievement Award as well as an Australian Water Association Merit Award for water cycle management (www.westhamfarmhouse.com.au).

Ian Kiernan at the Westham Farmhouse, NSW. Photo: Bob Seary

# foreword

Ian Kiernan, AO
Chariman, Clean Up Australia

Building, and the satisfaction of creating or restoring, is in my blood. In my youth I built canoes, boats and even furniture and soon embarked on a roller coaster of a career in the building industry.

By the mid '60s I had my own company, building everything from factories to commercial buildings as well as extensions to houses. I'd buy and renovate derelict houses in the then neglected areas of inner Sydney, installing new services and finding new uses – inadvertently preserving much of the city's early working-class heritage.

We had a staggering portfolio of nearly 400 terrace houses, commercial blocks and restaurants and when the credit squeeze of 1974 struck, I lost the lot! I left the building dream behind, and sailed out of Sydney Harbour for a year's adventure that took me on a life-changing voyage to thirty-six of the most beautiful Pacific Islands, along the way discovering the joy of solo sailing.

Fate, as it so often does, has another plan for you, and in 1986, I competed in the BOC Challenge single-handed around the world yacht race sailing the 18-metre *Spirit of Sydney*. The race course covered 27,000 miles and took the fleet around the Great Southern Ocean capes. One of the competitors encouraged us to hold our plastic waste on board for proper disposal when we reached shore as part of a school environmental project. Through this simple act, I started to see plastic everywhere – and realised just how much waste was ending up in the world's oceans. The builder who had once dumped his old roofing iron in the ocean, had seen the light!

Returning home, I saw Sydney Harbour with new, clearer eyes and decided to do something about the state of my own backyard, enlisting the help of Kim McKay, the co-author of this book and co-founder of Clean Up, along with a group of friends.

The rest, as they say, is history. Clean Up Sydney Harbour in 1989 was followed by Clean Up Australia and a few years later, Clean Up the World. Twenty years down the track, the environment and the impact of global warming has become the biggest challenge facing us all.

A fascination with architecture and historic buildings has always stayed with me and a few years ago, a friend showed me Westham Farmhouse, near Bathurst in New South Wales. Awe-struck by this example of convict-built Australian pioneer heritage, and even though the house was virtually derelict, I bought it.

Today the farmhouse and outbuildings are restored incorporating all environmental services circa 1830, overlaid with world's best environmental practice circa 2008. There's total water cycle management, solar power and hot water, biological waste management, recycled building materials and native plant regeneration. Westham's restoration has been a labour of love and is an example of how you can integrate environmental products and services into a working building.

*True Green Home*, created by Kim and fellow Clean Up director Jenny Bonnin, provides easy-to-follow tips and ideas on what you can do, whether you are renovating or building from scratch. Be inspired by what you can achieve – it could be the start of the change our world needs.

# introduction

Kim McKay and Jenny Bonnin

Since the release of our first book, *True Green: 100 everyday ways you can contribute to a healthier planet*, in 2006, environmental issues have taken front and centre stage globally. It's hard to escape news of the latest scientific findings on climate change, or the most recent way to reduce your carbon emissions, or which car to buy or eco-holiday to take. It can be confusing.

Some commentators are even claiming that there's too much information, which may contribute to a green backlash, and that the 'noise' created around these serious issues is in danger of overwhelming the public.

'Green noise' was recently defined by a *New York Times* writer as 'the static caused by urgent, sometimes vexing or even contradictory information played at too high a volume for too long'. Everyone seems to be saying 'just tell me what I need to know, just give me the cheat sheet'.

We're hoping *True Green Home: 100 ideas to help you create a greener home* will be the cheat sheet you're looking for.

Building or renovating a home is one of the biggest financial undertakings you'll face in your life and now more than ever, it's important to get it right. With Australia having the highest per-capita greenhouse emissions, we need to reduce our carbon footprint, and there's no better place to start than at home. Households contribute almost one fifth of our nation's greenhouse gases and the simple tips in this book should help contribute to a reduction.

We've both had experience at renovating homes – most recently a family terrace house (Jenny's) and a small apartment (Kim's), both near the inner city in Sydney.

We have tried to incorporate many of the practices and principals we've learnt during these renos, and others, into this book.

### Jenny's True Green Home Story

I'm a passionate renovator and have always supplemented my income by performing small building and decorative projects on inner-city terrace houses. The challenge has been to find properties where we can add value. Could parking be added via rear lane access, could a third bedroom fit into the roof cavity, was there any space to reconfigure the kitchen to include an internal laundry, second loo and a larger casual living area?

Whilst everything met council standards and appropriate architectural limitations, the main selling point was that the property presented extremely well, with clean lines and decorative touches from a 'I could easily live here and I don't need to do anything!' perspective.

Times are changing: green is definitely the new black when it comes to marketing homes and smart investments are getting smarter – literally. 'Smart Houses', 'Green Homes' and 'Sustainable Lifestyle Communities' are popping up everywhere.

I took all this on board, along with my passion and determination to make a difference, to be the change I wanted to see, and embarked on working with an architect to create a new green home.

Photo: Corbis Australia

It is very easy to find out about this from all our website resources at the back of the book but instinctively we all know what to do: we need to decide to live a less extravagant, more simple life, ditching unnecessary lifestyle props like air-conditioning and heated floors. It's easy to achieve natural airflow and temperature control by working out how to place your house on the land, where the windows are, and through the use of louvres, blinds and fans.

Energy saving is a great conversation starter – it's fashionable to know the solar water heater or photovoltaic system you have chosen, or how much rain is needed this season to accomplish water savings with a newly installed water tank. 'Going off the grid' doesn't mean you're dropping out of society but it does mean you are thinking in the right way and developing a sense of self-sufficiency.

I now spend evenings searching suppliers for recycled timber or sustainable timber for the floors, for low- and zero-VOC paint colour charts, energy-efficient appliances and native plants for the new garden.

When this house goes to market in time, it won't only be the design and decoration that will be the key for potential buyers. A sustainable house is the new trend and soon will become the standard – a 'true green home revolution'.

### Kim's True Green Home Story

I'm all about keeping my lifestyle simple, and with all the travelling I've been doing for work for the past 20-plus years, I decided that apartment living was the most practical for me. A few years back I found an old apartment with good bones and set about making it as energy-friendly as possible.

I have instant gas hot water, which saves on space and energy; energy-saving appliances; windows that remain open to take advantage of cross-breezes in summer; and even minimal overhead lighting – using lamps with energy-efficient bulbs to cut down on electricity usage. I used so little gas in the first 18 months that the gas company didn't even send me a bill! My simple renovation was cost-efficient too, as we kept the original floorboards, fixtures and fittings where possible.

I use gas heating during winter and one simple unit heats the entire apartment – I only have four rooms. My next challenge is to install a water tank and maybe even solar panels on the building – I better get active on the body corporate to see what can be achieved.

My home is compact and cosy. I call it my cubbyhouse and it's my retreat at the end of a long week, somewhere I can rest comfortably, knowing that my carbon footprint is shrinking all the time!

Have fun with *True Green Home* and let us know about your ideas for creating a sustainable home.

www.betruegreen.com

## Reduce your footprint

The average Australian household emits approximately 15 tonnes of carbon dioxide ($CO_2$) into the atmosphere every year. That makes Australia the number one emitters of $CO_2$ per person in the world – currently, we're even ahead of the USA and China. The challenge then for all of us is to change the way we live: to rely less on coal-fired power for our energy, to be more thoughtful about what we consume, and to use and recycle as much as possible so we reduce the amount of rubbish that ends up as landfill. To illustrate just what 15 tonnes of $CO_2$ looks like, we built a house out of wheelie bins: 15 tonnes of $CO_2$ = 340 x 240-litre garbage bins full each week!

The Brisbane Sustainable House, courtesy of Bligh Voller Nield Architecture. Photo: David Sandison

# home green home

# 1 location, location

This golden rule of real estate also applies to creating an eco-friendly home. By considering your property's location to public transport, school, shops and your work, you can significantly reduce your dependency on your car and add serious value to your home. Leaving the car at home and catching public transport, riding your bike to work and walking the kids to and from school all contribute to a healthier you and a healthier world. Whether you're renting, renovating or building your home, look for suburbs with established gardens and tree-lined streets that have good access to parks and open spaces to enjoy green vistas and increase the quality of your lifestyle.

Courtesy Environa Studio. Photo: Tim Wheeler Studios

# supersize (or downsize) me

2

How many rooms do you really need? The average Australian house size has grown to a whopping 264 sq m from 169 sq m back in the mid 1980s, according to figures from the Australian Bureau of Statistics. A big house is more environmentally expensive than a smaller one, regardless of its green efficiencies. Big houses can mean more furniture, lighting and cleaning, and longer commutes to shops, work and school. Be realistic about what you need, go for good design and energy efficiency over maximum square metres, and you'll be creating a house that's future proof against rising fuel and utility costs.

Photo: Corbis Australia

# the lie of the land

Building is an opportunity to make sure your property has its own green footprint for future generations. Consider how your property relates to the natural topography of the site. Choosing and using a site efficiently equals better energy efficiency. Understand the opportunities and limitations of your lot. Rectangular lots are generally more efficient in terms of land use, while sloping or steep blocks can require more excavation and fill and higher drainage costs.

Courtesy Environa Studio. Photo: Tim Wheeler Studios

# 4
# face up to it

The orientation of your home has a huge impact on your utility costs. Take your lead from the environment and create a green floor plan. Getting the best of the day's sun, the north side is not only brighter but also warmer in winter, and perfect for living areas. The west side's afternoon sun makes it a better choice for bathrooms, garages and laundries. The shady and cool south side is great for bedrooms, in warmer climates, or spare rooms. The east side, with its morning sun, is ideal for kitchens and bedrooms.

Courtesy Environa Studio. Photo: Tim Wheeler Studios

# material world

## 5

Think twice before you call in the skip, and avoid unnecessary landfill by recycling unwanted windows, bricks, timber, flooring and sheet metal in your reno or build, or by selling them to second-hand building specialists. Eco-friendly building materials are growing in availability and affordability. Ask your builder and architect to source green solutions to non-renewable resources such as: recycled timbers and steel reinforcements; engineered and plastic timber (great for decks); cement mixed with extenders; low- and zero-VOC paints, stains and finishes; and formaldehyde-free particleboard and plywood products.

Inverloch House in Victoria, by Solar Solutions Design. Photo: Matthew Mallett

# 6

# insulate yourself

With about 25 to 35 per cent of the heat gain in a house coming through the roof, and 15 to 25 per cent through the walls, good insulation is fundamental. Keeping you warm in winter and cool in summer, insulation will help to regulate your home's internal temperature by reducing drafts and leakage of cool and warm air. Insulation also improves the effectiveness of your existing heating and cooling solutions. Look for environmentally friendly and non-toxic insulation that will be good for the atmosphere in your home as well that of the planet.

Metricon Home, courtesy of BlueScope Steel

# 7 green design

From igloos to adobes, humans have created climate-sensitive designs to perfectly complement their geographic location. But in Australia, since white settlement, the building styles of European countries have dominated our landscape. The eaveless design, in particular, has been borrowed from colder climates, but is mostly unsuitable for the harsher Australian summers, where windows and rooms benefit from more shading. When designing or renovating your home, engage professionals who share your green vision. Choose architects, builders, plumbers, engineers and contractors that think green too. The cheapest quote is not always the best.

# passive attack

## 8

Banish the air-conditioner. Fresh air and natural light are essential for your health; invite them into your home, permanently, with passive design solutions and by reducing your reliance on electricity for heating and cooling. Create natural breezeways with the placement of doors and windows. Install skylights and enjoy free natural light for up to 14 hours a day. Venting skylights will improve airflow and air quality and prevent mould in bathrooms or laundries.

Courtesy VELUX Australia

# 9

# window shopping

With up to 40 per cent of your home's energy for cooling or heating being lost or gained through windows, improving their thermal performance reduces energy costs and greenhouse gas emissions. Windows and exterior doors need to be energy efficient and smart. The Windows Energy Rating Scheme (WERS) rates the energy impact of windows in housing anywhere in Australia. Consider the placement of windows to maximise natural light and create breezeways, and choose the right window for your environment. Double glazing is a good choice for freezing winters, providing less heat loss and less condensation. Louvred windows are great for catching the breeze on hot summer days.

# renovate or detonate

## 10

Weigh up the benefits of renovating an old property versus building a new one. There are 4.2 million homes in Australia that are over 20 years old – that's a lot of precious resources that can be renewed and updated. Older houses ad apartments have a lot going for them: great location, more character, quality timbers and established gardens. Have the best of the old and the new by restoring the detail, rethinking the floor plan for more modern living, and installing energy- and water-efficient appliances.

Courtesy CplusC Design. Photo: Adam Craven, Craven Images

# design for healthy living

**Every decision an architect, builder or homeowner makes can have an environmental legacy. Building a truly sustainable home is much more than solar power and rainwater tanks. The Brisbane Sustainable House, an elegant, contemporary Queenslander, is an inspiring example of a house with a minimal ecological footprint and with maximum environmental, social and economic sustainability.**

In 2004, Queensland celebrated the Year of the Built Environment with a national first, the Sustainable Homes Program, which saw more than 20 houses designed and constructed across the state's different climatic zones. An initiative of the state government and different local councils, the program's aim was to better inform the public and foster an understanding of sustainability, as well as influencing future public policy. The third project in line, Brisbane Sustainable House, went on to take a swag of awards for the builder Natural Lifestyle Homes and architects Bligh Voller Nield. In addition to strictly adhering to passive design principles and employing state-of-the art technology, the architects carefully selected low-VOC (non-toxic) products – including materials, flooring, cabinetry and paint.

Sustainable Homes project co-ordinator Stephanie Skyring highlights the sustainable design features of the house:

**1>** *Roof and ceiling design.* The indoor temperature has been stabilised through a natural air-conditioning system that draws hot air from both levels into the roof cavity and outside through clearstory louvres in summer, and draws warm air from the roof cavity into the house through a thermal chimney for warmth during winter. The thermal chimney and internal brick walls and stairs provide thermal mass, which equalises internal temperatures through day and night. Within the house, strategically placed louvres, multifold doors, and ceiling fans enhance direct and indirect cross-ventilation and air circulation to ensure a cooler, healthier indoor environment.

**2>** *Pest control.* In Australia, termites cause more damage to homes than fire, storms and floods combined, yet traditional chemical solutions to the problem can be

The Brisbane Sustainable House, courtesy of Environmental Protection Agency Queensland

an additional source of indoor air pollution. Sustainable Home avoids the need for these measure by employing physical barriers, including insect screens for windows and a stainless-steel mesh termite barrier.

**3>** *Building materials*. Sourced from renewable or recycled resources, where possible, all materials were carefully selected to ensure low embodied energy and low toxicity. All inbuilt joinery for kitchen, wardrobes, study and cupboards are zero or low in chemical toxicity.

**4>** *Paints*. Internal and external walls were finished with paints free from solvents and chemicals. Internal and external timber are preserved with oil-based finishes made from natural plants and minerals, and free from petrochemicals. All paints used on internal and external surfaces were water-based with zero VOC content.

**5>** *Natural flooring*. No carpets were used. Flooring from natural resources was selected instead, including bamboo flooring, crushed granite tiles for wet areas, and a modern linoleum, made from linseed oil, rosin and wood and cork flour. These options were chosen because of their high durability and low environmental impact.

green energy

# 11
# warm up with radiant heat

Nature uses it to warm us, and the Europeans have known about it for almost a century – radiant heating is one of the most energy-efficient and effective heating options available. By heating the floor, ceiling or panels in the walls of your house, you can achieve a more natural and consistent warmth. Other advantages over traditional convection-based systems and reverse cycle air-conditioning are that you're warming your whole house (not just one or two rooms), dust circulation is reduced (great for allergy sufferers), and those fights over who's hogging the heater become a thing of the past.

# you've got the power

## 12

Courtesy Todae (www.todae.com.au). Photo: Lee Stone

We are becoming increasingly aware of the running costs of everyday appliances like computers, televisions and refrigerators, but there are alternatives. Photovoltaic panels, which catch sunlight and transform it into energy, have been used on houses and commercial buildings for some time. Combine today's sophisticated panelling with Australia's sun-drenched climate, and it is possible to easily cover about 1500 kilowatt hours (kWh) a year. While the average Australian family uses around 5000 kWh, a house with energy-efficient appliances and using non-electric cooking, heating and hot water could need as little as 1000 kWh per annum.

# 13

# leave the heat outside

Ever admired those cute houses in Greece or Italy with their wooden shutters to keep out the sweltering midday sun? Well, there's a very good reason our Mediterranean friends have chosen this type of window cover. Outside awnings and blinds are much more efficient than their indoor equivalents, keeping temperatures down by up to 5 degrees. The iconic Australian verandah is perfectly suited to our hot climate, shielding the exterior walls and rooms of the house from the harsh sun as well as allowing additional ventilation on hot summer evenings.

Courtesy Environa Studio.
Photo: Tim Wheeler Studios

# 14
# clear the air

We all see our homes as a refuge from the pollution and smog of the city, but the air within our homes can be more polluted than outdoor air. Synthetic building materials, finishes and furnishings releasing outgas pollutants can harm your living areas. That lounge sofa you sit on every night might be more detrimental to your health than running along your city's largest street in peak-hour traffic. So do some homework on the materials you plan to use in your build or renovation and on those that are present in furnishings such as your carpets, couches, benches and wardrobes.

Photo: Corbis Australia

# 15
# nothing but hot water

Almost a third of our average domestic energy use is spent on producing hot water – 31 per cent, to be precise. By replacing your old electric hot water system with more energy-efficient options, you can make your single biggest contribution to the environment. Think about switching to gas or solar systems for your hot water needs; and if you can't do that, install a ruthless shower-timer clock that cuts the hot water supply.

Courtesy Ian Kiernan, Westham Farmhouse

# 16
# tanks for the free water

What could be more natural than harvesting the rain that falls freely from the sky? Considering an average family uses 240,000 litres of fresh water every year, half of which ends up down the toilet or in the garden, and you pay for it, installing a tank that can halve this waste seems an obvious option. Tanks can be small, huge, above or below ground. They can even be flat so you can use them as a fence or under decking – the new generation of tanks are far from ugly. You can also do it yourself: set out buckets, bins and old toddler pools to collect small reservoirs (under gutter pipes is a great location) and use them on your plants on the drier days. State and territory governments now offer rebates for installing new tanks, so it's definitely worth thinking about if you own your place.

Walkerville House, by Marc Dixon Architect. Photo: Lucas Dawson

green energy

# 17
# grey is the new blue

Don't just let all your waste water go down the drain. You can recycle it for non-potable (not for drinking) purposes with a readily available or more permanent grey-water recycling system. Grey water – that is, all non-toilet household waste water from baths, showers, washing machines and sinks – can be redirected, filtered and treated, to varying degrees, for additional domestic use such as flushing the toilet and specific outdoor purposes. Consult your plumber and your local council about the regulations, and health and safety considerations, of grey-water use in your area.

# recirculate hot water

## 18

It's frustrating, not to mention wasteful, waiting for hot water to flow through to the shower or tap from the hot water service. Waiting for just 30 seconds can result in 15 litres of perfectly good water going down the drain. But a simple hot water recirculator can pump cold water sitting in the pipes back to the tank until the hot water from the service is right at your tap. A system can be connected to every outlet in the house with just one pump, which uses only a small amount of energy. Check with your local government to see whether you are eligible for a hot water recirculator rebate.

The Brisbane Sustainable House, courtesy of Environmental Protection Agency Queensland

# 19

# phase out inefficient light

Join the Australian Government's initiative to phase out all inefficient light blubs by 2010. With lighting representing a significant amount of household greenhouse gas emissions, by installing, where you can, energy-efficient alternatives including compact fluorescent lamps (CFLs), you can make real energy savings. CFLs use only 20 to 30 per cent of the electricity of standard incandescent light bulbs to produce the same amount of light. The savings to you, the environment and the economy will be enormous – up to 4 million tonnes of greenhouse gas emissions alone (equivalent to 1 million cars off the road) and more than $50 per year for your household.

Illustration: Marian Kyte

# green rewards

## 20

Sign up with your energy provider and play a real part in increasing the production of renewable energy (such as solar, wind, low-impact hydro, landfill gas and bagasse) contributing to the national electricity grid. By signing up to a government-accredited Green Power scheme for a few extra dollars on your energy bill, your energy consumption can be converted into green credits so that you are literally investing in renewable electricity generation now and for future generations, replacing electricity generated from coal.

Photo: Marian Kyte

green energy 33

# an inspired view

> Striving to always combine creativity with practicality in her ecologically sustainable architecture, **Caroline Pidcock** believes passionately that Environmentally Sustainable Design (ESD) can be a potent influence in architecture, and vice versa.

When Pidcock started her own practice in 1992, sustainability was almost unheard of in Australia's architectural circles. Determined to set herself apart, and inspired by the emerging trends on other continents, she devoured literature about the subject and took up a teaching position at the University of Newcastle, where she imparted her passion to her students. More than 15 years down the track, her flourishing architectural office in Sydney employs nine staff and attracts many clients on the reputation of its sustainability agenda. Having been the president of the New South Wales chapter of Australia's professional body of architects, the Royal Australian Institute of Architects, and currently presiding over the board of the Australian Sustainable Built Environment Council, she is well respected in her field and knows her stuff. Yet she admits that debating and contemplating aspects of sustainable design and finding solutions to her clients' issues and needs still poses challenges and requires individual solutions. She says Australia's climate usually allows for a large portion of our everyday lives to happen outdoors. Especially in the warmer months and more tropical climate zones, backyards and verandahs are seen as an extension of the living room. This can make the climate control of indoor spaces a tricky business to attend to.

A few essential ground-rules apply when contemplating the design of your sustainable home. Caroline recommends:

**1>** *Don't cut corners*. See well-designed solutions for your doors and windows as an investment, and budget accordingly. Although energy-efficient solutions rarely pay back in the short term, in the long term your investment will be well and truly repaid. And remember, it is much cheaper to get things right in the first place. Retrofitting is always more expensive.

**2>** *A warmer view*. If you are designing a home from scratch, resist the temptation to put in too many windows and doors (although this can be very hard!). No matter which materials you use, well-insulated walls will always perform better when it comes to managing heat or coolness than doors or windows.

**3>** *Think smarter*. Consider a smaller home with well-designed and covered external spaces that essentially extend your living room.

**4>** *Cover-up*. All windows should have a well-designed cover to protect them from sun and rain. Also, make sure you can open your windows properly so you can circulate cool evening air during the summer months.

**5>** *Thermal properties*. When it comes to windows, make sure you have a good thermal frame. The standard aluminium frames aren't thermally broken, meaning they can easily transmit heat from inside to outside and vice versa. Make sure you do your research before you buy. If you are renovating or on a budget, be aware that you can find alternative products that have a similar effect as double-glazed windows.

green living

# 21
# room for room

Open plan living solutions are still all the rage for homeowners and builders alike, but think twice before you start envisaging that one large space for your entire family to live in. The more you are able to separate individual zones in your home, especially transitional zones such as hallways, the easier it will be for you to keep these areas warm or cool when you have to rely on heaters or air-conditioners.

Photo: Corbis Australia

# 22
# watch your step

A British study has found that about 40 per cent of the environmental impact we create in building our homes comes from floor finishes. Although it has good insulating properties, carpet can have a real environmental impact and exacerbate some health problems. Even pure wool carpet is often treated with chemicals to repel dirt and bugs. Try to source low-emission products, choose one with low pile, and clean carpets regularly to discourage dust mites, using a ducted vacuum. If you opt for timber flooring, make sure you source it from sustainably managed forests or timber recycling specialists and choose low-toxic natural finishes, like tung oil or beeswax, over plastic floor finishes such as polyurethane.

Courtesy Shiver Me Timbers

# light my fire

## 23

We love the romance of a fireplace in winter, but fireplaces and wood-burning heaters can contribute up to 40 per cent of air-particle pollution. Check your heater complies with the EPA standard, it is installed correctly, and you are using it efficiently – closed, slow combustion heaters are best. Ensure that your wood is from a sustainable source. Wood smoke contains pollutants that can be harmful to your health, so use old and dry wood as it burns cleanly and efficiently; don't let your fire smoulder overnight or use it to burn household rubbish. And have your chimney or flue professionally cleaned before each winter for maximum safety and efficiency.

# beat the draughts

## 24

Your home may have survived its share of renovations and design fads but they do leave their scars. Beware of pulling up old carpet only to reveal large gaps between the floor and the bottoms of doors where doors were ordered specifically or shortened to allow for carpet. Revive the humble door snake and use rugs on gappy floorboards. Draught-audit your home. Find green solutions to deal with other culprits such as gaps in walls and skirting boards. Ensure skylights, exhaust fans, downlights and chimneys are fitted professionally to minimise DIY-related draughts. Seal your windows and doors properly to prevent as much as 25 per cent of heat losses and gains.

Courtesy Shiver Me Timbers

# your biggest fan

## 25

Ceiling fans are an attractive, quiet and inexpensive option for your cooling and heating needs. They work by circulating cool or warm air around the room and run at about one cent per hour, compared with 12 cents for evaporative cooling and up to 60 cents per hour for refrigerated air-conditioning. And the energy saving is considerable too. Place containers of ice under ceiling fans in summer to create a cool breeze.

*The Brisbane Sustainable House, courtesy of Environmental Protection Agency Queensland*

# 26

# don't stand by

Standby power can cost the average Australian household as much as $50–100 a year. When appliances are left on standby, they are not off. This wasted energy accounts for as much as 10 per cent of all household electricity. The simplest way to save is to turn them off at the wall. Just switching off your computer, television and CD player properly can save around 115 kilograms of greenhouse gas emissions every year; and you'll save even more if you turn off all your gadgets. Ensure you have power boards with individual switches so you can isolate items you use less often, and use standby sparingly, to retain your settings on specific appliances.

Photo: Corbis Australia

# 27
# let the music play

Your beloved stereo can be energy consuming but you can offset this by choosing equipment from manufacturers with a green procurement philosophy: using recycled, non-hazardous construction materials and minimal packaging. You can also reduce waste by refusing to be lured into constant upgrades, and recycling whenever you can. It's been estimated that 2.39 kilograms of materials are used in making just one CD. Reduce the load by going digital and storing music on your computer or digital media player – and don't forget to turn off the standby mode.

Photo: Corbis Australia

# 28

# star performers

With the equivalent of 2.4 televisions per Australian household, and the changes in technology over the last decade, your TV has become a major culprit of greenhouse gas emissions behind refrigerators, space heaters and coolers, and water heating. But unlike them, TVs are not regulated by a star-based energy rating program to help you make the greenest choice. Not yet anyway. The Australian Government is considering the case for introducing energy performance standards and comparative energy labelling. In the meantime, be aware that your groovy new plasma or LCD wide-screen telly may fail a green test.

Photo: Corbis Australia

# 29 window dressing

Adopt your grandmother's decoration tips and dress up your windows with curtains, blinds, shades, awnings and shutters to instantly improve the thermal properties of your house. These old-fashioned measures are not only back in style, but will minimise heat loss and draughts in winter and keep the hot sun out in summer – all further reducing your heating and cooling bills. Some things don't even cost you money: closing the curtains at dusk will stop heat escaping through your windows, for instance; while in summer keeping your house closed up in the mornings will retain the cooler night air until the cooling breeze arrives in the evening.

Inverloch House in Victoria, by Solar Solutions Design. Photo: Matthew Mallett

# 30
# don't get sucked in

Australians bought 1.13 million vacuum cleaners in 2006, and the number is increasing every year – which raises two questions: what are we doing with all those old cleaners, and how many vacuum bags go into landfill? Invest in a bagless cleaner to reduce the waste, and choose a machine with a long warranty, so you're not adding it to landfill after just a few years. If it breaks, get it repaired. Clean filters and tubes regularly to maximise energy efficiency.

Photo: Corbis Australia

green living

## understanding space

> Less is more encapsulates the essence of sustainable design as practised by Victorian designer **Luke Middleton**. No matter how sustainable, biodegradable, environmentally friendly or recyclable the materials used in your home or renovation, nothing beats not using them at all.

Middleton's design firm, EME Group (that stands for ecologically motivated environments), has carved out a niche in the refurbishment of small to medium-sized offices, which incorporates not only the structural design, but also the branding and performance of his clients. However, the Melbourne-based designer and his team apply their skills to a spectrum that ranges from developer-driven multi-residential buildings to family homes. It even incorporates the odd media appearance, such as ABC-TV's *Carbon Cops*, where Middleton consulted a family on the design of their energy-guzzling family home, which was subsequently entirely revamped and will now be built according to EME Group's blueprint. Having studied both construction management and architecture, Middleton gained hands-on construction experience before launching his architectural career. He suggests that a thorough understanding of materials is the key to sustainable design practice, and that even a very beautiful design should be derived from pragmatic considerations, rather than driven solely by aesthetics.

'Everything should be there for a good reason,' says Middleton, as he shares five key issues behind his design approach:

**1>** *Think ahead.*
The first step to true sustainability is building less. That means to understand each space in your home and how it will be used now and over time. For instance, you might not want a whopping lounge suite in your living room, so it can be smaller, or you might find that building central hubs instead of hallways will save a lot of space.

**2>** *Look around.* Don't just look at your own home. When you build, extend or renovate, take surrounding properties into consideration. Bordering your garden onto your neighbours' will psychologically increase the space. Situating your home to the wall of an existing building will increase thermal mass and decrease heating requirements.

**3>** *Keep it real.* Use natural materials and keep them that way. For instance, there's no need to paint ceilings or to cover up floors. Exposed natural materials will look contemporary for years to come and require minimum maintenance.

**4>** *Stop the drips.* It's best to save and store your water, but here, the devil is in the detail. Take a good look at your taps – do they use too much water to begin with? The difference that water-saving fixtures and good habits can make is enormous.

**5>** *Buyer beware.* Watch out for false claims, greenwash – it's rife. Read the small print and never forget to query the attributes of a product: How much embodied energy did it use? Is it locally sourced? How does it relate to other products in the field? Talk to sales staff and don't be afraid to ask too many difficult questions.

# 31
# green gourmet

Choosing new kitchen cabinetry will present you with a real green challenge, but set yourself some basic rules – like sourcing materials locally, avoiding particleboard and fibreboard, and insisting on low-VOC cabinetry. Benchtop materials should be durable and water-resistant; stained concrete or indigenous stone are good options. Alternatively, source a recycled kitchen from a recycling centre or online, and customise it for your needs. Mix and match with new products if you can't find exactly what you want second-hand.

# 32
# fridge magnets

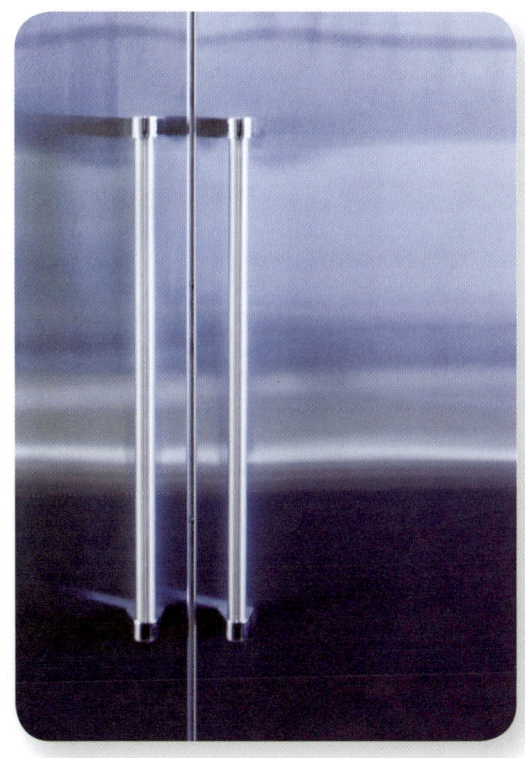

Fridges are a central part of our modern lives, but they are one of the biggest energy-consumers in the home. The average household fridge consumes around 950 kWh per year, a second refrigerator uses 830 kWh, and a freezer uses 650 kWh, generating around 1.4 tonnes of $CO_2$ every year. Reduce consumption by improving your fridge's efficiency. Buy a machine with a good energy rating, and don't buy one that's too big for your needs. Install it in an airy place away from other heat sources (eg the oven); this can avoid up to 150 kilograms of greenhouse gas each year. Check your fridge's operating cost on the Federal Government's Energy Rating site (www.energyrating.gov.au).

Photo: Corbis Australia

# ye olde fridge

## 33

Old-model fridges are up to 50 per cent less efficient than new ones. But if you're stuck with an older model for a little longer, first congratulate yourself for not contributing to whitegood waste; then there are a few simple things you can do to reduce your running costs and make it more efficient. Keep the thermostat at a suitable level so you're not wasting energy on freezing temperatures. If the fridge is near a window, draw the curtains to keep the sun off it. Clean the condenser coil (usually at the back of the machine) and make sure the seals on the doors are maintained. When you go on holidays, empty it and turn it off, leaving the door slightly ajar.

Photo: Corbis Australia

# the wash-up 34

An efficient dishwasher can use half the water of average models. Ensure your dishwasher isn't power hungry by considering good energy and water efficiency label ratings (WELS). By 2016 the WELS system could save nearly 1200 megalitres per annum in national dishwasher water consumption – enough water to fill 600 Olympic swimming pools each year. With about 80 per cent of the energy required to operate a dishwasher devoted to heating water, choose a model that allows you to reduce the amount of hot water used. Opt out of the automatic drying mode and choose fast or economy cycles when you can. Only use the dishwasher when you have a full load.

Photo: Corbis Australia

# 35 in the oven

In Australia, ovens (both gas and electric) are yet to be labelled for consumers with an energy efficiency rating. A staggering up-to-90 per cent of the energy used by the oven is wasted – so consider alternatives like the microwave, an electric frypan or a pressure cooker. Use your oven efficiently: ensure the seals are tight so that heat doesn't escape, and make sure the inside light works so you don't have to open the door too often to check on your roast or cake. Go green and avoid using toxic chemicals to clean your oven; alternatively, wipe it down with a soapy cloth when it's still warm, fill a roasting tray with water and heat the oven on medium until the water is almost evaporated, then wipe down and scrub stubborn spots with baking soda.

Photo: Corbis Australia

# 36
# check what's cooking

As a rule of thumb, gas cooking only generates half or even less of the energy generated by electric cooking. However, electric induction cooktops can be 50 per cent more efficient than electric hotplates, so consider this option when it's time to get a new one. Just putting lids on saucepans and simmering food gently rather than boiling vigorously can make a big impact. Remember that each litre of water boiled off generates up to a kilogram of $CO_2$. With our great climate, make more use of your barbie for everyday meals, as cooking outside immediately saves you from having to switch on lights and exhaust fans.

Photo: Marian Kyte

# 37
# making waves

Microwave ovens are very efficient cooking appliances, largely because they use a relatively small amount of energy to achieve the required results. Choose an appliance with automatic sensor controls, a rotating turntable or stirrer fan and a computerised control panel to ensure precise cooking time and power. Keep in mind that looking after your microwave will help it last longer: a unit with a ruined waveguide cover (which may spark or burn) is expensive to fix because of the labour involved, and many machines get thrown out because of this. Ensuring this part is kept clean, as per the manufacturer's instructions, can extend the life of your appliance.

Photo: Marian Kyte

# around the hood

## 38

Without an over-stove exhaust fan, an average 4 litres of cooking fat a year will end up on your walls, ceiling and cupboards. Rangehoods are great for ridding the air of grease, steam and odour – which can also reduce your repainting time – but they can be major energy-eaters too. Choose a unit with fluorescent overhead lights, which last longer than traditional halogen ones, and ensure it's installed between 60 and 80 centimetres above the stovetop for maximum efficiency. If you have a recirculating hood, as opposed to a ducted one that transfers air outside, make sure you clean the outside filter as well as the inside carbon filter regularly.

Photo: Corbis Australia

# 39
# make a splash

Splashbacks are a popular choice to protect surfaces around sinks, stovetops and food preparation benches. But the traditional tiled splashback, particularly those tiny mosaic styles, can be a nightmare to clean without resorting to chemical cleaning products. Explore other design options that will be easier to keep clean – such as stainless steel, glass, laminate, larger tiles, marble or granite – and where possible source off-cuts, second-hand or recycled options.

Courtesy Shiver Me Timbers

# tools of the trade

## 40

Ensure that everything in your kitchen can last a lifetime, avoiding unnecessary disposal in toxic landfill. Don't buy cheap tools that can bend, break or melt quickly. Invest in quality plates, serving dishes, baking equipment, pots and pans. Choose energy-efficient toasters, kettles and other gadgets with long warranties. Wooden spoons can be rejuvenated and sanitised by a good boil in a pot of water. Invest in tight-grained wooden chopping boards from recycled or sustainable sources, and ensure their longer life by oiling them down with linseed or olive oil; rather than soaking them, sand them (and oil again) when knife cuts look deep.

# material choices

> Before you plan that feature wall and get out those colour palettes and carpet samples, take on board the advice of an expert. University of New South Wales' **Kirsty Máté**, program head of Interior Architecture and director of Eco Balance, a company consulting to designers and organisations on issues relating to design and sustainability, suggests longevity is a crucial factor that's often overlooked in home design.

Máté familiarised herself with sustainable interior design during a stint working as a designer in Germany in the late 1980s, where environmental design was already high on the agenda. Returning from the land of recycling and reusing, she channelled her newfound passion into the Society for Responsible Design in Sydney, an organisation that helped designers acquire skills in this burgeoning area. At a time when the internet was still in its infancy, finding information wasn't always easy. 'People thought we were mad,' Máté recalls. 'No one knew what we were on about when we spoke of VOCs and the like.' In 1987 she started her business, Eco Balance, consulting to designers and organisations keen to apply sustainable design principles. Máté believes there is still some way to go in Australia to increase the awareness and usage of sustainable design, particularly in interior fit-outs. 'So far, people have focused on the building envelope, and such things as solar energy and water conservation,' she notes. The design of corporate spaces increasingly needs to employ aspects of sustainability, as companies become more aware of the effects pollutants can have on air quality and, consequently, on productivity.

She's been actively involved in the research and promotion of sustainability and design since the early '90s, so take note of Máté's golden rules for renovators, new builders and home decorators:

**1>** *Reduce the quantity of materials you use.* Often, it is not really necessary to splurge on extra materials or on extra finishes. Consider the amount of different materials used to produce your flooring or wall covering. For instance, if the floor of your home consists of a concrete slab, there is often no need to apply extra flooring or carpet. A concrete base provides excellent thermal mass. Equally, laminated flooring or wall coverings require glue, whereas timber floors don't.

**2>** *Selecting materials so they best fit your purpose.* High-maintenance materials such as carpet require a lot of chemicals in their production and maintenance. Take the example of the concrete floor: using too many additional floor or wall coverings can render the thermal qualities of another material redundant. Also, think about wear and tear. High-traffic areas in your home need to be very carefully considered so they don't continue to gobble up resources in their maintenance.

**3>** *Selecting materials that are benign in their environmental impact.* Find out how products were manufactured and how they were treated. This can be very confusing, so eco-labelling schemes such as Good Environmental Choice and Eco Specifier are perfect for saving you time and energy when doing your research. You are never comparing apples with apples, so leave the final material selection up to the experts.

**4>** *What's cheap is usually cheap.* Select your products for reuse and recycling. Poor-quality products will wear quickly and cannot be sold again, whereas high-quality furniture or building materials do not tend to lose their value as quickly. Don't be afraid to ask where products and materials came from, who made them and where, and what substances were used in their manufacture.

**5>** *Ask yourself a critical question: do I need that, or do I just want it?* Work out if it is really necessary to throw out your entire kitchen to achieve the look you want, or would it be enough to just reshuffle and acquire a few new things. Work out if you really need a separate room for each activity, and look at flexible building systems to allow for change in the family.

# bathroom basics

# 41

# hot water systems

Almost a third of the greenhouses gases we create each year are in the production of hot water, yet much of the energy is wasted due to heat loss along pipes and tanks. You can minimise this waste by making sure your pipes are well insulated and your hot water unit is as close as possible to the place where you'll need it most. When choosing a new hot water system, get one that suits the needs of your family. The larger the system, the more heat it will lose and the less environmentally sound it will be. Avoid a system with a continuous pilot light, as powering a pilot light can release up to 200 kilograms of greenhouse gases each year. Try not to use hot water if cold will do. Put a bucket in the shower, to catch the cold water while you wait for the hot water to kick in, and use it on your pot plants or garden.

The Brisbane Sustainable House, courtesy of Environmental Protection Agency Queensland

# waterworks

When choosing new fixtures and appliances for the bathroom (and laundry), make sure you base your decision on the Federal Government's Water Efficiency Labelling and Standards scheme, which rates water fixings such as taps, showers, washing machines and toilets with up to six stars for maximum efficiency. From 2008, all new products should sport the WELS label. The label shows you the product's star rating (water efficiency) as well as its water consumption – for example, 13 litres per minute – so it's really easy to choose the best items for your bathroom. Check the WELS online products database to compare the ratings of water-using equipment (www.waterrating.gov.au).

# 43

# sink or swim

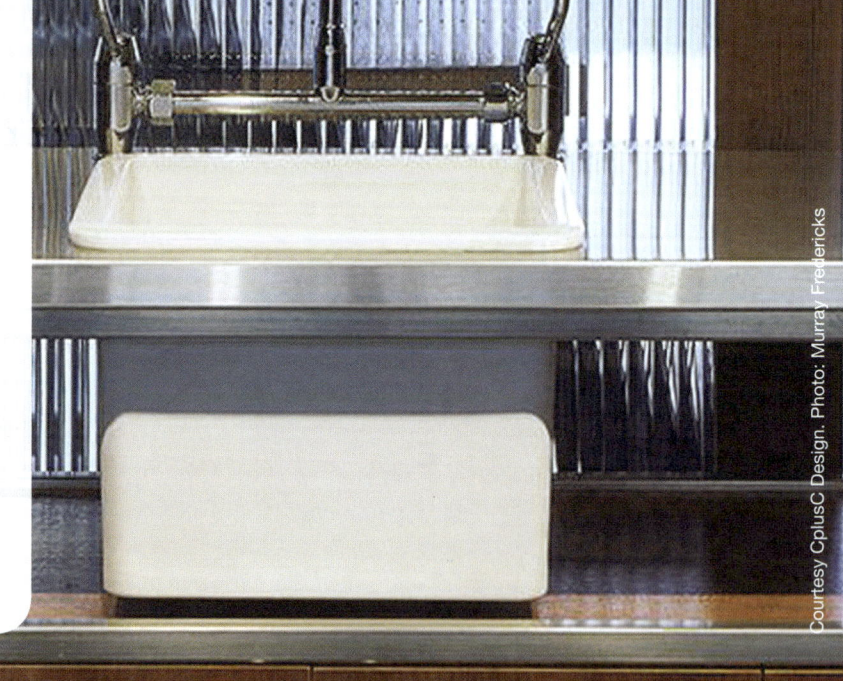

Don't let the tap run and waste our most precious resource as part of your family's daily bathroom rituals. Embrace the humble plug and use your basin as it was intended, by filling it with some water to wash your hands and face or to shave. Don't run the tap when brushing your teeth – use a cup of water instead. Any of these simple ideas can save as much as 5 litres of water a minute. Check that your plugs are actually keeping water in the basin, as leaky plugs equals water wasted.

# 44
# recycled fittings

If you're updating your bathroom, give some thought to where new materials come from and the amount of energy used to produce them. There are lots of opportunities to source stylish recycled and no-longer-wanted bathroom fittings rather than buying new, mass-produced, energy-intensive items. You can now get ceramic floor tiles made from recycled windscreens, and retro basins and cast-iron baths are readily available. Ensure your cupboards and benches are derived from sustainable (rather than old-growth) materials. Check your telephone directory or the internet for recycling centres and other options.

# 45

# flushed away

Toilet flushing is responsible for about one third of all water used by the average Australian household, which means that 78 billion litres of quality water is flushed away every year. Upgrade to a true Aussie innovation with a star-rated dual-flush toilet; without one, your single-flush loo can use up 12 litres in one flush, compared to a dual-flush's 6 litres or less. Check with your local council – you might even be able to switch to a waterless composting toilet. If you're stuck with your old dinosaur, place an inexpensive toilet dam (available from your hardware store) in the cistern to reduce the amount of water in each flush, or fill an empty soft-drink bottle and place that in the cistern. Silent leaks can waste up to 225 litres a day: drop a little food colouring into your tank and wait 15 minutes – if the colour turns up in the bowl, call your plumber.

The Brisbane Sustainable House, courtesy of Environmental Protection Agency Queensland

# reading matter

## 46

That two-ply designer toilet paper is indeed an expensive luxury. According to the Australian Conservation Foundation, every tonne of paper recycled saves 13 trees, 2.5 barrels of oil, 4100 kilowatts of electricity, 4 cubic metres of landfill and 31,380 litres of water. But only 5 per cent of toilet paper used in Australia is recycled – the rest is made from plantation or native forest trees. Make the switch to environmentally friendly recycled toilet paper that is unbleached, chlorine-free or 100 per cent recycled.

# light showers

## 47

Showers are the biggest users of resources in the home, but you can reduce this just by spending less time in the shower and using a timer. You'll save up to half a kilogram of greenhouse gas for every minute. Replacing your old showerhead with an energy-efficient one, with at least three-star/AAA rating, can save you around 10 litres of water a minute. Take advantage of rebates and offers provided by the government, your council or water provider to make the switch. Keep a bucket handy to collect the grey water for use in the garden. Install a thermostat that keeps hot water at a useable temperature so no cold water is wasted.

Courtesy Interbath Australia

# 48

# in the tub

Many Australians are simply getting used to showering instead of bathing, since a bath uses up to 150 litres of water compared to a possible 40-litre shower. But there are occasions when a bath is indispensable, such as for therapeutic reasons or when bathing a child. There are still a few things you can do to reduce water and energy consumption, though: bathe the kids together, insulate around the tub or install an in-line heater to keep the hot water hot, and you won't have to constantly refill. After their bath, use that grey water for the garden, and make sure to get the kids involved.

Courtesy VELUX Australia

# 49
# pick up the steam

It is essential to have an exhaust fan in your bathroom to reduce mould and other harmful contaminants, but that's no reason to forget the fan's negative environmental impact. Choose energy-saving exhaust fans that are thermostatically controlled and not connected to the light switch, so they turn on when the air temperature rises rather than when anyone puts on the light. Clean the fan's filter once a month to ensure that it runs efficiently.

# eco-accessorise

## 50

Make your washing area an eco-friendly haven with a few small changes to your bathroom basics. Toss out that PVC plastic shower curtain in favour of a natural alternative, such as a 100 per cent organic hemp or a heavy cotton one, that doesn't cost the earth (literally) in its production and is more naturally resistant to mould. Update your bathroom linen with organic cotton towels. Choose earth-friendly soaps and cosmetic products. That plastic bathmat can go too, in favour of a washable cotton alternative. And don't forget to recycle bathroom containers for shampoo, conditioners, bubble bath, mouthwash and so on.

Photo: Corbis Australia

# easy ways to modify

> You don't always have to build afresh to make your home sustainable. Modifications can be done to all homes, house or apartment, old or new, or even rented. An expert in sustainable conversions, **Jeremy Davies** shares some of his sustainability wisdom.

Problem solving, designing and fixing things has always been a passion for Davies, an engineer at heart, who now heads the impossibly cool online eco superstore Neco. Focusing on selling sustainable home products and offering a consultation service to businesses and homeowners on their eco-material choices, Neco had its beginnings when Davies bought an investment property in the late 1990s off the plan, and he was surprised to find that no environmental considerations had played a part in the design of his house and land package, so he set out to source his own features that would make this home sustainable. Fast forward to 2008, and Davies – now a walking, talking encyclopaedia when it comes to anything sustainable around the home – and Neco advise private homeowners and businesses on how to minimise their ecological footprint.

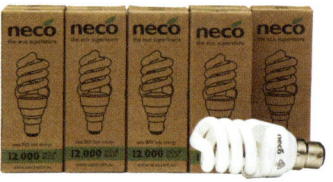

Neco's vision and values are firmly based on their philosophy to make your world a better place. Here are Jeremy's must-do's in building or renovating your home:

**1>** *Esky your home with proper insulation*. For new homes, government-introduced schemes now stipulate that you have to have a certain amount of insulation; however, it is wise to go above and beyond the minimum amount required for your climatic zone, and really try to make sure there are no gaps or holes. Adding a little more won't cost you much more, but will make sure that your home can – depending on the season – keep heat out or in much more efficiently. Also, under-roof insulation (the stuff that sits directly under the roof tiles, not on the ceiling) is currently not mandatory, but it really pays to add another layer there.

**2>** *Invest in double glazing.* Whatever your situation, there are solutions to ensure maximum window insulation for every budget. Ideally, it's best to have double-glazed windows installed, but there are products available that will attach to your current window frame and create and additional – almost invisible – barrier, trapping air between the glass and a new membrane in the same way that double-glazing works. The extra bonus: you still get to enjoy those treasured heritage features, such as stained-glass windows and the like.

**3>** *Don't do downlights.* The small lights have become the standard in many new houses and renovations, but even though you might furnish them with energy-efficient light globes, a light source is a light source and will use extra energy. You simply don't need that many lights. Concentrate on one central light source per room, and additional ones for night-time reading and the like.

**4>** *Curb the light outside.* Most people believe they need a lot of outdoor lighting, when they actually don't. Replace that 50-watt halogen light outside with a simple, one-watt LED, and you'll only use a fiftieth of the energy. Beware of the solar-powered outdoor lights. Low-quality ones might soon deteriorate and become landfill.

**5>** *Invest in water solutions.* Water tanks are no longer big unsightly things more at home on a farm-sized property. Rule number one is to get a large one installed, because a small one will run out quickly, and who knows when it will rain next. The best possible way to fit a large water tank is to install an underground one. This might not be within the scope or budget if you are only renovating, but there are other solutions. New, flat water-panels are as thin as a standard fence and can even be used as one, along the side of your property. With enough panels, you might still be able to fit a 3000-litre tank without too much trouble. Supplement your water tank with a grey-water treatment system and you might never have to tap into the water mains again. An average family will then be able to reclaim as much as 300 litres per day.

sleeping green

# 51
## step lightly

**G**iven that you spend more time in your bedroom than just about any other room of your house, don't ruin your pristine sleeping environment with volatile wall finishes or flooring. Opt for environmentally friendly paints on your walls and flooring. Choose solid wood, bamboo or recycled cork over vinyl flooring; natural-fibre rugs and mats that have not been treated with stain-resistant finishes are good choices. Check the labelling on wood stains and polishes – anything containing wood-preservative chemicals in the active ingredients should be avoided.

Courtesy BT Bamboo flooring, supplied by Eco Flooring Systems

# a natural mattress

## 52

Synthetic materials used to make mattresses are not only energy-intensive to create, but they are also not biodegradable and add to problem waste. They can contain harmful glues, foams, pesticides and flame retardants. Natural fibres, however, have built-in protective properties, and readily absorb and release the moisture we emit while we sleep, so they're less likely to attract dust mites and bacteria. Look for products made from wool, organic cotton, latex and sustainably harvested wood. Air out natural-fibre mattresses in the sun – this will kill dust mites and other organisms.

# 53
# make your bed

Choose bed bases and bedroom furniture made from solid wood – either second-hand, reclaimed or from sustainable forests – or other sustainable products such as bamboo. Plywood and chipboard consist of wood pieces held together with toxic glues; they can be less structurally sound than solid wood and may not last as long. Moreover, the source of plywood and chipboard is often untraceable, and the materials may come from old-growth forests – irreplaceable treasures that are being lost at a rate of 32 million acres a year. Support manufacturers who follow a green procurement policy and look for products displaying a Good Environmental Choice Eco-Label.

# between the sheets

## 54

Make the switch to organic sheet sets for a sounder sleep. Conventional cotton is a water- and pesticide-intensive crop with significant environmental impacts across its production, manufacturing and processing. Support positive change in the industry by updating your linen cupboard with certified 100 per cent cotton bedding that is unbleached, chemical-free and uses vegetable-based dyes. You can also get sheets made from hemp or bamboo, both of which require far less (if any) pesticides and herbicides to grow. Hundred per cent cotton is a much better bet than polycotton.

sleeping green

# eco-air freshner 55

There is a simple way to dilute the pollutants that build up in your home – all you need to do is open the windows! The accepted rate of air change is one per hour, which indicates the number of times that the entire volume of air inside the house is exchanged with the air outside the house. Keep your fresh air from windows really fresh with natural-fibre curtains and blinds. Organic cotton, wool, flax (linen) and hemp drapes are good insulators, naturally long-lasting and strong, and natural dyes are more fade-resistant than synthetic ones. Don't forget about the benefits of using house plants throughout your home. From the bathroom to the living room, house plants are nature's own air fresheners, removing toxins and unhealthy air pollutants and adding to your living space.

Courtesy VELUX Australia

# pillow talk

56

Your lungs and skin will breathe more easily with natural-fibre (not synthetic) pillows, blankets and doonas. You can get pillows made from latex, organic cotton, wool and buckwheat, doonas made from wool as well as feather and down, and beautiful cotton and wool blankets. Synthetic fibres are not only ineffective and encourage chemical production, but they trap air and water near the skin and make for uncomfortable sleeping – especially for small children. Don't forget to use healthy and sustainable doona and pillow covers. You can wash pillows, doonas and blankets in your washing machine, adding a few drops of tea-tree oil to kill off dust mites; fluff and air them out in the sun to dry.

Courtesy Neco and EcoLinen

sleeping green

# cotton on

We've all stayed in hotels where those polite signs in the bathroom suggest you hang up your towel so you can use it again, to save precious water and energy. Many hotels claim around 70 per cent of guests happily opt to do this and in doing so help to achieve at least a 5 per cent reduction in energy usage. It's a good idea at home too. Fresh-air drying your towels each day will cut down on the number of times you need to wash them. You'll just need to train the teenagers in your household to pick up damp towels off the floor and hang them out to dry. And remember to only buy 100 per cent organic cotton towels when you update your linen press – they also make great gifts.

# 58
## storage dreams

Good storage systems are key to a nice comfortable bedroom. Look for options made from recycled wood and steel – you need them to be strong so they'll last. And you don't necessarily need custom-built storage: customise old furniture yourself by removing or adding shelves or drawers, and use your imagination when it comes to stackable crates and boxes that can be readjusted as your mood or circumstances change. Remember to store off-season clothes in breathable containers such as rattan trunks or muslin bags. Cedar chips with a couple of lavender-oil drops on them are a safer alternative to pesticides such as naphthalene moth-repellent products (eg mothballs).

Photo: Corbis Australia

# 59 changing rooms

Chances are, the home that suits you today won't suit you tomorrow. Australia's 2006 census has shown that across Australia, more than a million three-bedroom houses are occupied by just two people. A room that's a bedroom this year might not be one in the next. When you plan your home, make sure that a room that's a designated bedroom could also serve well as a study, library or guestroom, or could even become part of another area of the house through demolishing a wall. Flexibility in your design can help reduce emissions and materials.

Courtesy VELUX Australia

# 60
# keeping your cool

When building from scratch or renovating, remember that the bedroom is the room in the house where constant temperatures are most important. Passive design principles and a few clever decisions make this possible even in the hot summer months. Ensure walls (especially western- and eastern-facing ones) are insulated, while roof overhangs, awnings or vegetation should shade the house. If it's more than one storey, contemplate having your bedrooms on the ground floor. High ceilings allow hot air to rise above the living space and ceiling fans to be placed at the right height, while vents over doorways and high-positioned windows enable hot air to escape.

# the art of sitting down

> It's true that furnishing a room can be like investing in a beautiful wardrobe. And those cheap knock-offs are just that – doomed to do your back in and fall out of fashion. **Ewan McEoin**, of Studio Propeller, an independent media and marketing consultancy, recommends you invest in a classic design, locally made and certified accordingly, to give you that wow factor and years of comfort and pleasure.

If anyone knows about good furniture in Australia, it's Ewan McEoin. He's the former editor of *(inside)* Australian design review, co-editor of the Sydney and Melbourne Design Guides and currently director of Studio Propeller. He's also artistic director of Victoria's peak design event, State of Design 2008, as well as Springboard, an initiative to educate and promote local designers. A passionate supporter of Australian design, Ewan has contributed widely to national and international design journals and sits on several design panels and groups throughout the industry.

Having studied environmental science in a former life, sustainability in design is very close to McEoin's heart. So take his advice on selecting, buying and enjoying furniture, and follow these fundamental rules:

**1>** *Think quality*. Even without investigating how a product is made, where it came from and what materials it comprises, a well-made piece of furniture that will last a long time is always going to be a sustainable product to some extent, simply because it won't end up in landfill after five years. A quality upholstered piece of furniture can be re-upholstered after a decade and look brand new.

**2>** *Look for certification*. If the piece of furniture you've got your heart set on is made from wood or has wooden components, then look for an environmental label. Products carrying the Forest Stewardship Council

Stak Stool and Leda Seat, courtesy Jon Goulder

(FSC) label are made by companies who care about the environment and purchase their timber from sustainably managed plantations. Chances are, those companies take the same care in purchasing all their other materials.

**3>** *Buy local.* Australia's furniture industry produces fantastic products made by talented designers around the country. They might be a little more expensive than product that was cheaply manufactured in China, but what you'll buy is originality, sustainability and a good portion of local pride.

**4>** *Consider buying classic second-hand furniture.* You can buy a classic second-hand designer piece for about the same price as a new piece of furniture. Think about the style and design-savvy you'll exude. Much better than showing off the couch with that complicated Swedish name that's in almost everybody's lounge room.

**5>** *Avoid cheaply made products with a lot of artificial components.* Although some quality products use high-end biodegradable plastics, most inexpensive plastic furniture will deteriorate much quicker than a product made from timber or metal. And quick deterioration in plastic products means hitting the landfill – restoring these products is rarely worth the trouble.

# 61
# breathe easy

In Australia, more than 80,000 tonnes of VOCs (volatile organic compounds) are released into the atmosphere annually, paint being a large contributor to this figure. Choose low- or zero-VOC paints, stains and primers rather than oil-based products. Manufacturers can provide material safety data sheets (MSDS) listing ingredients and their possible impact. If you're renovating a property built before 1970, test it for paint containing lead. Know the safety precautions you must take when working with lead-based paints, by reading the free government booklet *The Six Step Guide to Painting Your Home* (www.environment.gov.au). Research natural-fibre wallpapers, made from bamboo, sisal and straw.

# 62 roll on up

When repainting your home, get your painting estimates right to avoid having paint left over. This will not only cut down on the clutter in your garage or backroom, but also help the environment and your renovation kitty. Most hardware stores will help you find out how much paint you need. Just make sure you measure up all of the wall and ceiling spaces before you go to buy paint – and don't forget to deduct the window and door areas from the total figure.

# 63 classics

When it comes to buying furniture, one of the best things you can do for both your wallet and the environment is to buy pieces that will last forever. While it may seem a little steep to fork out all that money for your dream chair when your car registration is due, just save a little longer and you can afford timeless, quality pieces that won't end up in the landfill. Have your chairs and couches re-upholstered to update your interiors. Also, look out for good second-hand options that can be restored to their former glory.

# 64
# ethical style

More and more manufacturers of furnishings are making commitments to green procurement and manufacturing standards. When you are decorating your home, make it your business to know what you're buying and who you are buying from. Check the labels. Do your research and don't be afraid to ask too many questions to be sure your piece of furniture also has a green conscience. Only when you know where the materials came from, what they were treated with and who made them should you purchase the furniture. That way you can be sure you're not encouraging unethical or unsustainable production.

Courtesy CplusC Design.
Photo: Greg O'Conner, Red Dog Design

# 65
# mood lighting

There's nothing more charming than dimmed light to set the mood of a room, but for soft and non–fossil fuel lighting try a few candles. Avoid spending money on over-packaged, artificial-fragrance paraffin wax products that are derived from crude oil and emit carbon dioxide. Beautiful beeswax candles are much more environmentally friendly and are often available from a local supplier; plus you can add a personal touch with a few drops of essential oils – much more romantic. Pure soy wax candles are another healthy and natural alternative to paraffin wax candles. Soy wax is also easier to clean if spilt on fabric: with a little rubbing and warm soapy water, it's gone.

# refreshing air

## 66

Reduce the air pollution in your home by airing your house regularly. Choose environmentally friendly products to keep your home smelling fresh – why use artificial room deodorisers, especially those that require electricity, when you can just open a window and use the sanitising effects of sunshine and fresh air to reduce food and pet smells? Or make your own non-chemical, cheap room deodorisers, by mixing a teaspoon each of baking soda and lemon juice, or just a few drops of an essential oil you like, with two cups of hot water in a reusable spray bottle.

## 67
# safe-home office

Australians send 34 printer cartridges to landfill every minute. That comes to 2040 an hour, 5000 tonnes per year. However, it's easy to reduce unnecessary waste by watching your printing use, recycling your empty cartridges responsibly in the bins provided at office supplies outlets, or having your empty ink and toner cartridges refilled. Reduce the possible risk of any laser printer emissions that may be harmful to your health and ensure that you home office is well ventilated to allow airborne particles to disperse.

# 68 reduce e-waste

About 98 per cent of discarded televisions, computers and mobile phones become e-waste, dumped in landfills. Many of the items contain dangerous materials including mercury and cadmium, which can leach into landfill sites and eventually the water system. E-waste is growing at five times the normal waste rate – the fastest growing stream of waste in the western world. The response to this is: repair, reuse and recycle. Fix repairable items, reuse working components, and source specialist recyclers (eg www.recyclingnearyou.com.au, www.cleanup.com.au/au/campaigns/mobile-phones). Failing that, donate your old computer to charity or use a registered recycling facility (eg www.greenpc.com.au, www.vic.computerbank.org.au).

Photo: Corbis Australia

# 69
# the paperless home

Ever heard of the paperless office? You can make a difference in your home by applying green workplace principles to paper conservation. Scan and keep documents electronically rather than in paper files. Opt to pay your bills and do your banking online with your bank and service providers. Research has shown that to pay a bill by cheque, 2.87 kg of materials need to be displaced and shifted, while paying online needs only 0.26 kg – the calculation that looks at these things is called material input per service (MIPS). Use recycled paper in your home printer, always print on both sides, and use old paper for scribble pads.

Photo: Corbis Australia

# 70

# non-stationary stationery

Everyone uses pens, pencils, pins and packaging at some time, and you can make the most out of these products by thinking about them as permanent, not disposable, items. 'Disposable' pens are not disposable – more than 10 billion plastic pens end up in landfill around the world every year. Bring some style back into your note writing by investing in a good-quality reusable pen (where you only need to buy ink). Reuse envelopes and packaging and choose reusable items whenever you can, including tape dispensers and pencils. When buying stationery, think recycled: you can purchase pencil cases made from car tyres, rulers and personal organisers made from old juice cartons, pencils made from plastic cups, and mouse mats made from recycled circuit boards.

Photo: Marian Kyte

CASE STUDY

# the good life

> When **Pierce Cody** had an hour to kill in New York's SoHo district, he found – and consequently brought to Australia – a new approach to food shopping: a store that's more like a community rather than a shop. According to Cody, living healthily and sustainably means engaging with the products we buy and eat, and above all to develop a healthier attitude toward a sustainable lifestyle.

Cody's stores, Macro Wholefoods Markets, hover deliciously somewhere between a traditional health food store, a supermarket, a health clinic and a deli. The stores include cafes and offer naturopathy, yoga and massage facilities – catering to all facets of customer well-being with the aim of bringing the organic lifestyle into the mainstream. Macro Wholefoods aims to convert sceptics to a more holistic way of living, challenging people to rethink their attitudes to grocery shopping and diet.

Cody says his customers are far from typical health food nuts. Coming from every sector of society, they share one common motivation: they want to feel good about their shopping choices without giving up their lifestyle.

Riding high on the sustainability wave, Cody's approach to his business is driven by the idea that making informed and healthy choices in a happy environment creates happier customers, and in turn, a happier planet. He

Courtesy Macro Wholefoods Market

seems to be on the money. Since 2005, the eight-branch chain that stocks over 12,000 products has expanded and Pierce is looking forward to opening 40 stores around the country in the same successful, accessible format. Cody believes it is possible for everyone to contribute to both our own and the planet's health without having to sacrifice our lifestyle or constantly feeling guilty about our indulgences. And here are his tips for a holistic lifestyle:

**1>** *Choose wisely.* The lifestyle choices you make should be ones that make you happy, not ones that make life more difficult. Remember that living in an environmentally sustainable way genuinely makes you feel proud about yourself and the decisions you make.

**2>** *Educate.* Make sure the kids are on board – help them understand that every time they leave a light, TV or computer on they are contributing to the problem.

**3>** *Go organic.* Get the whole family involved in do-it-yourself organic gardening. Compost, mulch and manure are the best and easiest ways to combat poor soil and water restrictions, and to produce your own organic produce.

**4>** *Switch off.* Standby is not an option – turn your appliances off at the power point.

**5>** *Walk.* Stop using the car. It's a great way to spend time with the family, think about your lifestyle, enjoy the environment and reap the personal benefits of exercise.

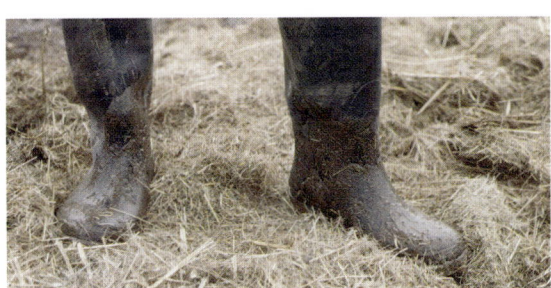

# green housekeeping

# 71
## care for your clothes

A staggering 77 million wire clothes hangers end up as landfill every year. Don't just throw yours out when you bring home the dry cleaning – why not take them back to your dry cleaner for reuse, give them to your local charity shop or even save them for craft projects. If you're in the market for new ones, seek out eco-friendly, recyclable alternatives made from recycled paper or cardboard. Buy long-lasting wooden hangers from recycled or sustainable sources, or old ones with a bit of character from second-hand stores.

Photo: Corbis Australia

# 72

# pressing issues

If you feel that ironing is a waste of time and energy, try avoiding it altogether with some simple tricks. Use the cold water cycle on your washing machine (it's heat that causes the wrinkles in the first place); wash light clothing in one cycle, heavy in another (so the weight doesn't squash your delicates); bring laundry in from the line while it's still damp, so the sun doesn't 'dry' wrinkles into the clothes; and hang clothes on hangers so they retain their shape while drying. When you do iron, it makes better energy sense to do it in lots rather than piece by piece, and avoid wasted energy by not overheating the iron.

# 73

# the natural finish

Contrary to all those advertisements, you don't really need a different cleaning spray for every piece of furniture. Apart from creating more packaging and placing extra strain on the environment, the mineral oils and chemicals contained in those products are also a major contributor to indoor air pollution. Clean furniture with a damp cloth. It's a bonus if your furniture is made from untreated timber, because then you'll be able to use maintenance products made from natural oils and beeswax, creating that beautiful smell.

# 74
# carpetbaggers

It's important for your health to keep your carpets clean as they can trap dirt and mould and harbour dust mites. But make cleaning your carpets a more environmentally friendly process. Commercial carpet cleaning generates waste water that includes chemicals and dirt from the cleaning process. Clean your carpets with environmentally safe chemicals and natural alternatives (eg salt for red wine stains) and employ green-aware carpet-cleaning professionals. Why not place small, washable rugs made of untreated natural fibres over your carpets, or check out other flooring material such as bamboo squares.

Photo: Corbis Australia

# 75
# wipe out chemicals

Over 300 man-made chemicals can now be found in our bodies that people weren't exposed to just three generations ago, but we still aren't sure what effect these chemicals are having. Reduce your possible exposure to any harmful chemicals in your everyday cleaning by using eco-friendly cleaning ingredients and methods. Your whole bathroom can be cleaned with a bit of bicarbonate soda, some vinegar and that old staple – elbow grease. Substitute natural germ fighters such as tea-tree or eucalyptus oil for bleach and chlorine, and reduce the amount of cleaning needed by regularly wiping down wet surfaces so that grime doesn't build up. Always choose detergent that is biodegradable with low phosphorus content.

*The Brisbane Sustainable House, courtesy of Environmental Protection Agency Queensland*

# shine your kitchen

## 76

You simply don't need to buy a lot of harmful chemical products in wasteful packaging to clean your kitchen and utensils. There are books on natural cleaning – browse your local bookstore to find solutions such as the following. For silver that's really tarnished, soak it in a solution of hot water, baking soda and a dash of dish soap. For copper, try polishing with equal parts of tomato and Worcestershire sauce. Brass comes up a treat with equal parts of vinegar and salt. Rub baking soda into tea and coffee stains, and clean benchtops and sinks with a microfibre scourer and a bit of baking soda.

# scrub up

## 77

A lot of soap and body-cleansing products contain high amounts of synthetic materials, which can be harmful to the environment and your skin, containing possible pollutants, allergens and irritants. There are plenty of products now that use organic or all-natural ingredients, or you can make your own. The internet is a great source of homemade recipes using readily available ingredients. You could even collect soap bar remnants in a dispenser and just add water to make liquid soap.

# 78

# ease the load

Front-loading washing machines use less water than top loaders, which can mean 70 per cent less water or 36,000 litres per year for a typical household. They also need less detergent and consume less electricity. Look for machines with at least a four-star energy rating (the highest is six), always wash with a full load, and choose detergent that is biodegradable with a low phosphorus content. Also, heating the water for a hot wash generates up to 4 kilograms of greenhouse gas, but you'll generate less than a third of a kilogram of greenhouse gas per wash using cold water – so switch to cold washing and reduce water heating and greenhouse gases by 80 per cent.

# 79
# it's a wrap

In this era of containers being available in so many shapes and sizes, there should be little need to add to landfill by using plastic wrap, paper or disposable plastic. Get sandwich-shaped containers for lunches and take reusable containers to take-away outlets and delis. When it comes to refrigerating leftovers, transfer them to tubs with lids or cover bowls with a plate rather than using foil or plastic wrap.

# that sinking feeling

## 80

Check all the taps around your house. New taps have energy star or A-ratings – more stars or As means less water waste – and you can get flow restrictors or aerators fitted to existing taps (aerators lower the flow by adding air to the stream). Check for leaks and replace washers regularly – a leaky tap can dribble away up to 200 litres a day – and be sure to turn off taps properly or be prepared to see up to 600 extra litres of water a day appear on your bill! Keep plugs in the sink when washing fruit and vegies, and use the water later for rinsing dishes or watering your indoor plants.

# smart planting

> Your backyard is your own private world. It's the best place to start making a real difference to our environment. Elaine Shallue, project co-ordinator for Sustainable Gardening Australia, explains the art of growing your garden with realistic and sustainable alternatives to conventional gardening practices, in tune with nature and the seasonal rhythms of the land, its ecology and its climate.

Sustainable Gardening Australia (SGA) was borne out of the realisation that the gardening industry had an ethical responsibility towards the home gardener. An idea that started six years ago through an initiative of Environs Australia, Bulleen Art & Garden and the University of Melbourne, SGA now runs a thriving suite of workshop programs for amateur gardeners and continues to provide environmental certification to a long list of landscape professionals and nurseries in Victoria, Tasmania, South Australia and Western Australia. By 2008, more than 100 nurseries across four states have vowed to follow more sustainable business practices and educate their clients about sustainable gardening. Shallue explains that SGA's central purpose is to provide information.

'Sustainable gardening is about biodiversity, organic soil management and minimising the use of artificial chemicals and fertilisers,' Elaine says, adding that the most important element of a sustainable garden is a holistic approach to planting and following some core objectives in setting up a sustainable garden:

**1>** *Work with the lie of the land*. It's one of the simplest principles but one that people tend to miss. It is important to see your existing soil as a canvas to work with, selecting and matching plants to suit the conditions. Terracing or levelling can disrupt natural cycles, and by being equally aware of surrounding gardens, trees, bushland and natural waterways, gardeners can ensure that their patch of land becomes part of a larger eco-system.

**2>** *Be realistic*. Determine your needs and then set up your garden accordingly. If you don't have kids or a dog, you don't need a large lawn. In the days when we were allowed to water our lawns, up to 70 per cent of water was used for lawns. People who have installed rainwater tanks should seriously consider this, as their painstakingly collected $H_2O$ will be mostly used to keep the green from going brown, rather than growing and

Courtesy Sustainable Gardening Australia

maintaining other plants. In garden planning, make enough room for practical spaces, like worm farms and compost. A garden is more sustainable if green waste from gardening and kitchen scraps are composted on-site and don't have to be transported off-site to be treated.

**3>** *Consider your environmental footprint*. Remember that once in landfill, green waste can be worse than ordinary household waste, as it produces methane gas, which has 21 times the greenhouse warming potential of carbon dioxide. When treated at home, green waste still produces some carbon dioxide, but no methane. Consider carbon sequestration. Most people believe that becoming carbon neutral means planting trees, but also by organically managing our soil, we can contain the carbon in the ground rather than releasing it.

**4>** *Don't overdo it*. Reduce your dependency on fertilisers, but instead recognise the limitations of your soil and plant accordingly. Research shows that gardeners tend to over-fertilise. In a sustainable garden, the only area that should need some (organic) fertiliser is the vegetable patch. Remember too, not every insect is a pest. As a matter of fact, less than 1 per cent are, so learn as much as you can about all plants, birds and insects in your garden. Once you've identified pests, identify green ways of keeping them under control. Coffee grinds get rid of snails; decoy plants and companion planting will distract pests.

**5>** *Be diverse*. Make biodiversity work for you and get your mix of plants right. By incorporating mixed plantings you will greatly reduce the risk of pests and fungal diseases. A truly sustainable garden will also incorporate some food plants; to reduce food miles, feed the family and provide many physical and mental benefits.

# 81
# going native

Many Australian gardens feature introduced plants that aren't suited to the Australian climate: they can require a lot of water, soil additives and pesticides to really thrive. Or worse, they can escape your garden and become an invasive pest. Growing your region's native plants is a great way to ensure minimum water usage and maximum gardening success, because these plants are meant to be there. Ask your council for a list of natives, to restore the natural habitat of your suburb, starting with your own backyard. Or ask your local nursery for advice on plant types from similar climates that will work well.

# 82

# compost

Australians toss out around 3.3 million tonnes of food every year – that's a quarter of our actual food supply. But recycling your organic and green waste literally gives you something for nothing: your own 100 per cent organic fertiliser for your garden that will improve your soil, its water retention and the vigour of your plants, by delivering to them much-needed nutrients like phosphorus and nitrogen. Large gardens can keep great compost heaps going; if you have a courtyard garden or are in an apartment, source a system suitable for indoors.

Photo: Corbis Australia

a greener garden

# worm your way in

83

While your average garden worm won't quite get you there or do the job, you can establish a thriving worm farm in an unused corner, with a few stackable, modified crates, some compost and newspaper, and some Red Wrigglers, Indian Blues or Tiger Worms from your local nursery. If well maintained, your farm's population will double every two or three months. The basic idea is that worms dig upwards to fresher food scraps, leaving debris behind that makes incomparable fertiliser for the vegie patch. You can enquire at your local council for inexpensive start-up kits.

Photo: Corbis Australia

# chicken little

## 84

If you have the space, keeping a couple of chooks in your backyard not only provides a great source of fresh, free-range eggs, but letting them out to roam and forage for a few hours a day will help keep the pests in your garden at bay. Each chick also generates around 100 kilograms of superb organic fertiliser every year. Grab some four-by-twos and a roll of – you guessed it – chicken wire, and spend a weekend with the kids building the family a little chook run. There are plenty of plans on the web, but you should check with your council for regulations and advice about keeping chickens.

Photo: Corbis Australia

a greener garden

# 85

# mulch it up

Reduce erosion and the amount of water your garden needs by mulching regularly. Adding a layer of organic material to your garden beds reduces evaporation by up to 70 per cent, reduces weeds and improves the quality of your soil, making your garden even healthier. Choose 100 per cent certified organic mulch over inorganic options or save some money by using your own grass clippings, fallen leaves or shredded newspaper. You'll need enough to cover the soil in a layer at least 5 centimetres thick. Ask your council or local waste disposal facility about mulch deliveries.

Courtesy Sustainable Gardening Australia

# 86
# edible garden

Agriculture is a big user of fossil fuels. The fruit and veg in the supermarket may have travelled thousands of kilometres to make it to your table, not to mention the associated costs of packaging and storage. Support local market gardeners and suppliers or revive the vegie patch in your garden and plant some fruit trees to source your own truly organic produce. From a large-scale vegetable patch to herbs grown in pots on a balcony, you can grow small amounts of fruit and veg to supplement your needs. There's plenty of organic gardening advice on the web, and ask your council about local gardening groups you can join.

# 87

# friendly plants

In the wild, many varieties of plants grow in the same location, sharing their resources to help each other thrive. Use the principles of companion planting and let nature do some of the hard work of helping your garden thrive and stay pest-free. By researching and planting the right combinations of plants, you can naturally control pests by attracting the right insects and discouraging the wrong ones. Insects, after all, are natural recyclers, pruners and composting machines.

# bird life

## 88

Birds are great caterpillar and bug eaters, and making your garden a safe and pleasant habitat for them is easy. Provide fresh water by installing a bird bath or pond, and plant indigenous trees and shrubs to give them a natural food source, such as nectar. Build your own nesting box out of recycled materials or find one at your nursery and you'll be doing your bit for biodiversity. Use some old netting or chicken wire to keep birds away from seedlings and fruit. Avoid the use of garden sprays and poisons such as snail bait, and don't let your cat (or your neighbour's) roam around the garden.

Photo: Corbis Australia

a greener garden

# 89
# be water-wise

The days of hosing your garden for hours on end or setting up the sprinkler to give the lawn a good soak are well and truly over, and for good reason. Save water and reduce watering bills by creating and maintaining a water-wise garden. One of the best investments you can make is to install a drip irrigation system that delivers water directly to the roots of the plants. Design your water-wise garden with plants suited to your soil and weather conditions. Regularly check your outdoor taps, pipes and plumbing fixtures for leaks. One dripping tap can waste 2000 litres a month.

Photo: Corbis Australia

# 90 pest control

Avoid the overuse of synthetic chemical fertilisers and pesticides in the care of your garden. They don't discriminate between good insects and pests; moreover, they can be harmful to you and your garden's wildlife, and ultimately can contaminate our waterways. By using some commercially available pesticides you may also inadvertently be party to any adverse environmental impacts in their manufacturing process. Try organic pest remedies, such as mixing one tablespoon of vegetable oil with three cloves of crushed garlic, leaving it to soak overnight; then strain the mixture and add it to one litre of water and a teaspoon of liquid soap, before popping the result in a spray bottle. Rinse all produce, homegrown or shop-bought, before use.

a greener garden

# going solo

> An average Sydney household uses approximately 700 litres of water a day, mostly drawn from the public water supply. It was too much for **Michael Mobbs**, whose renovation led to the creation of Sydney's Sustainable House, a nineteenth century inner-city terrace which has provided all its own water, sewerage and energy needs for over 10 years.

In 1996, it was time for Mobbs and his family to renovate their inner suburban Sydney home. An environmental lawyer, he was keen to add some features to make their abode more sustainable. So when he started to research, he soon realised that it was possible to stop relying on public water and electricity supplies, and instead install water tanks, solar panels and water and sewerage treatment systems that would mean he and his family would be entirely self-sufficient. Mobbs estimates that he spent roughly a third of his budget on sustainable features, which would have been even less if the house had been built from scratch.

By 2013 the family will most likely have recovered their $50,000 of expenses through saving on bills and rates, and now have a truly sustainable house for the future. Here's how Michael Mobbs did it:

**1>** *Water security*. Firstly, an 8500-litre concrete tank was installed underground, beneath the family's deck. Rainwater from the roof is directed here, with overflow going into a mini-wetland area in the family's backyard. Enclosed drainpipes and sieves prevent leaves and debris getting into the tank. The water, about 100,000 litres per year, is used for drinking, cooking and showers. It is just enough for a family of four who use water wisely, and would suit two people with the average Sydney water usage.

**2>** *Waste management*. Another tank under the deck looks after the waste water and sewage. Unusually long and narrow, the tank was custom-built for the site and also catches food scraps and biodegradable waste. The sewage works its way through three layers of filter beds, consisting of sand, peat, live worms and bugs. Cleared by these organisms, the water is filtered in much the same way as rainwater naturally is. Then, it's ready to be used for flushing the toilet, washing clothes and watering the garden.

**3>** *Grey water*. Bugs and viruses contained in the water are further eliminated through a UV radiation zapper, which is solar-powered so it uses no electricity. About 270 litres of water per day are used as grey water.

**4>** *Solar-powered*. In the Mobbs' case, 18 solar panels on the roof supply about 60 per cent of the electricity to the house, but with extremely energy-efficient appliances, this could be considerably less. With improving photovoltaic technology, as well as more such panels, a house could be entirely self-sufficient when it comes to electricity. However, disconnecting from the electricity grid is never a good option, since excess solar electricity can be diverted into the system, thus private households can become electricity providers and even make some money while they're at it.

**5>** *Hot water*. A further solar system also heats water. Unlike the photovoltaic system, it relies on the heat of the sun, rather than its light. A gas booster helps out on rainy days. Together, the house's solar panels and hot water system generate enough power to save about 6 tonnes of coal from burning in an electric power station, thus preventing 20 tonnes of greenhouse gases from being released into the atmosphere.

around the house

## 91 a cool house

One of the most efficient ways to keep your house cool inside isn't even in the house! Trees and plants that provide shade can significantly reduce the heat that penetrates your home, with direct sunlight generating as much heat as a single-bar radiator over each square metre of surface. Judiciously planting some trees and shrubs around your home can reduce the intensity of the sun on the eastern and western sides of your property, long-term. The clever use of deciduous trees can mean that you enjoy the warmth of the sun in winter and protective shade in summer.

# outdoor lighting

## 92

We love our backyards, and outdoor lighting is great for extending the enjoyment of your garden into the evening, but it can also be a huge energy-eater. Check out solar-powered lighting, which will charge during the day and emit a lovely glow at night. If you're after a more powerful lighting source, install timers or sensors so that lights aren't left on overnight; don't over-light areas, but do install switches to control individual lights.

The Brisbane Sustainable House, courtesy of Environmental Protection Agency Queensland

# 93

# pave the way

Why not turn that high-maintenance lawn into a low-maintenance paved area? Did you know that using a powerful mower to cut the grass for an hour causes the same amount of pollution as driving your car for over 500 kilometres? Rethink the expanse of your lawn. There's heaps of paving options available, including recycled products, and paving means less watering, less mowing and less general maintenance. Scatter a few potted plants around your paved area to keep the garden spirit alive.

Photo: Corbis Australia

## 94
## over the fence

When thinking about a new fence, go for long-lasting, recycled and environmentally friendly treatments. Reusable fence posts and palings can be purchased from recycling facilities (formerly known as 'tips') and second-hand building suppliers. Buy new materials from sustainable sources like bamboo and plantation timber. Wire fences are also available second-hand or constructed from recycled metals. If you're just after a simple garden or pet fence, recycled plastic ones are available from hardware stores. Prolong the life of your fence by protecting it with non-toxic pest and rust deterrents.

# 95 cover the pool

With water restrictions in place throughout Australia, there are limits to how and when you can fill or top up pools and spas. So, if you own a pool, think about installing a water tank to fill it. Ensure your pool filter is the right size for the pool and is working correctly, so it's not consuming energy unnecessarily. Maintain the surfaces and check for leaks – a source of up to 7000 litres of wasted water a year. Invest in a pool cover or blanket to save on heating and cooling costs, as well as water evaporation.

# 96 playtime

You don't need to entertain the kids with energy-intensive, mass-produced play equipment. Use old tyres (which are an environmental nightmare to recycle) for swings; old, untreated timber for sandpits; and recycled wood and furniture for cubbyhouses. You can buy second-hand playground equipment and gym mats made from recycled materials. Choose water toys that use water from rain tanks and containers.

around the house 125

# out of sight out of mind

## 97

There is considerable debate about the environmental impact of PVC pipes commonly used in domestic plumbing, particularly their end-of-life disposal and the associated issues of landfill, incineration and recycling. Weigh up the benefits of polyvinyl chloride versus PVC-free alternatives like HDPE (high-density polyethylene) for your plumbing needs. HDPE pipes are readily available and are easy to use for the environmentally aware builder, and it has a much higher recycling rate to recommend it.

*The Brisbane Sustainable House, courtesy of Environmental Protection Agency Queensland*

# recycling rules

## 98

It has never been easier to recycle, and nowadays over 82 per cent of Australians regularly participate in kerb-side recycling. Support your local council's efforts to ensure we have a rubbish-free environment. Your council will offer free information and advice, as well as regularly serviced bins for green waste, rubbish and recycling including opportunities for the safe disposal of household chemicals and larger household rubbish. Create your own recycling centre in your own home with a few well-placed containers: one for compost, one for recyclables, one for materials for the kids' craft projects, and one for rubbish. Dedicate an area in the kitchen for the waste bins; it doesn't have to be huge, whatever suits your needs.

Photo: Corbis Australia

# 99
# green clean your car

Cleaning the car is a weekend ritual that shouldn't be left un-greened! Avoid the use of chemical-based car polishes and detergents. There are new, waterless cleaning products on the market or you can adapt your household green-cleaning kit to your car (using bicarb to deodorise your car's carpets, for example). Don't use the hose – washing your car with hose in hand can waste around 180 litres of precious water. Ideally, wash your car with a bucket of water on the grass, not in the driveway, so that your lawn can benefit from the extra water. And there's a good argument for letting the pros do it for you, as long as you choose a carwash that uses biodegradable, non-toxic detergents and recycled water.

Photo: Marian Kyte

# 100
## shine on

Make room for a clothesline around your house, preferably in a sunny and windy spot. Using a machine to dry your clothes three times a week can cost you $100 a year and produces more than 3 kilograms of greenhouse gases per go. Yet most people have access to a solar-powered drier in their own backyard: the sun. Clotheslines don't have to be ugly and obvious – there are many options that fold down and away. If you do need a drier, go for one with a high energy-efficiency rating, and make sure it runs properly by cleaning the lint trap regularly and checking that the machine has adequate airflow. Set up a winter clothesline under a covered area to dry your laundry on rainy days.

around the house

# the bigger picture

> For **Frank Fisher**, Australia's Environmental Educator of the Year 2007, being truly green doesn't mean to mechanically change our behaviour, but to address the systems that drive how we think and act. He suggests that contemplating the bigger picture even for the smallest decisions is the only way to achieve true sustainability – today and in the future.

In 1979, Frank Fisher, a trained electrical engineer, became Victoria's first full-time lecturer in Environmental Science when he took up the post teaching a Masters program at Monash University. To the thousands of students who have since come under his tutelage, Fisher hopes to have imparted not only knowledge and awareness of environmental issues, but what he refers to as 'systems thinking' – an ability to see and change the larger structures that cause environmental and social problems. 'This means exposing contradictions and misrepresentations that become apparent once we begin looking at the world through sustainability-sensitive lenses,' Fisher says, adding that 'asking someone to change this is a tall order, especially when you start doing things differently and realise you are not necessarily supported.' Doing things differently is something Fisher has a lot of experience in. Often referred to as a social activist, the prolific author continues to cultivate strong relationships with the media. He has created headlines for big propositions, like introducing the world's first free public transport in Melbourne, and for smaller but no less powerful endeavours, such as producing so little household waste that his week's rubbish would fit into a milk carton.

As far as advice goes, Fisher is adamant that the problems of the world won't be solved by following a how-to rulebook, but by people learning to examine each problem, recognising and questioning the larger constructs behind it, and finding the best solution for themselves.

'Look at it as if your patterns of living mattered, not the detail. The options are liberating,' he asserts, illustrating his point by challenging us to reconsider five basics of our modern lives:

**1>** *Rethink the car*. The first and most obvious point is to tackle our obsession with the car. It gives us security and comfort, evident in the size of SUVs that populate our roads. A simple calculation shows how wasteful this obsession is. Car engines convert 15 per cent of the energy available in their petrol to motion. The rest is heat, which is part of the reason cities are warmer than the countryside. Few want to ride engines. Engines push cars and together they are some 15 times heavier than drivers; so only one part of that 15 per cent moves the driver; 14 per cent move the car. Beyond that, energy is the energy required to make, maintain and dismantle cars

Photo: Marian Kyte

after their dash is done. Still further is the energy to make the infrastructures cars drive in, and to repair the damage they cause us and the environment. And still we drive.

*2> Rethink the fridge.* When it comes to refrigeration, we should begin to reduce our needs by not simply buying more energy-efficient fridges, but by challenging our cooking and food storing expectations. Our requirements to run refrigerators will not change until we contemplate the way we purchase, prepare and keep food. Is it necessary to store large amounts of food? Does everything need to be refrigerated? Remember that one commercial refrigerator is proportionally much more efficient that a smaller, household one. It's more efficient to go shopping more often (if you don't drive to the store, that is) and prepare foods that do not require much refrigeration.

*3> Rethink the bin.* Begin to reduce your waste by looking at the size and weight of your waste bin. Then contemplate what is unnecessary waste and tackle this at the source. Use your mind and question the necessity of every single bit of packaging. It starts with small steps like taking your own containers when getting take-away food, and telling the vendors that you'll take the responsibility for it.

*4> Rethink the source.* Contemplate where the food you eat comes from and what you could do to change its impact on the environment. Sometimes, solutions are simple, like eating raw sugar instead of the refined product, which consumes a lot of energy in preparation, with the end product being exactly the same. What's important is that each product should be contemplated separately. There are no hard and fast solutions.

*5> Rethink your routine.* Realise the culprit behind many of environmental crimes we commit is habit. Our task is to identify these habits, contemplate them, and then change them. What would happen if your light switches were at knee height, and you'd have to bend down to turn them on or off? Can you introduce markers in your environment that make you pause, recognise and question your habits?

# websites

**Green building resources & industry organisations**

| | |
|---|---|
| Housing Industry Association – HIA | greensmart.com.au |
| Green Building Council of Australia | gbca.org.au |
| New Zealand Green Building Council | nzgbc.org.nz |
| Sustainable Homes Program Queensland | sustainable-homes.org.au |
| Buy Recycled Business Alliance | brba.com.au |
| 5 Star House | 5starhouse.vic.gov.au |
| Building Sustainability Index | basix.nsw.gov.au |
| Sustainability Victoria | sustainability.vic.gov.au |
| Smart Housing | Build.qld.gov.au/smart_housing |
| Efficient Windows Collaborative | efficientwindows.org |
| Archicentre Architectural Services | archicentre.com.au |
| Earth Building Association of Australia EBAA | ebaa.asn.au |
| Australian Council of Building Design Professions | bdp.asn.au |
| Building Designers Association of Australia | bdaa.com.au |
| Permaculture Research Institute of Australia | permaculture.org.au |
| Association of Building Design Assessors | absa.net.au |
| Australian Green Development Forum Agency | agdf.org.au |

**Green homes**

| | |
|---|---|
| Michael Mobbs' Sustainable Home | sustainablehouse.com.au/location |
| Sustainable Home Brisbane | Sustainablehomebrisbane.com.au |
| Low energy living | lowenergyliving.com.au |

**Tools**

| | |
|---|---|
| Ecological Footprint Calculator | epa.vic.gov.au/ecologicalfootprint/ |
| Nationwide House Energy Rating Scheme | nathers.gov.au |
| Water saving program and calculator | thinkwater.act.gov.au |
| World Resource Institute Safe Climate Calculator | safeclimate.net/calculator |
| Emissions Calculator | elementree.com.au/calculator |

**Green labelling**

| | |
|---|---|
| Window Energy Rating Scheme | wers.net |
| Good Environmental Choice Program | geca.org.au |
| Water Efficiency Labelling Scheme | waterrating.gov.au |
| Energy Star | energyrating.com.au |
| Fairtrade | fairtrade.com.au |
| Forest Stewardship Council | fsc.org |
| Green Globe EC3 | greenglobe.org |
| Greenhouse Friendly | greenhouse.gov.au/greenhousefriendly |
| ISO 14000 | 14000.org |
| Green Power Accreditation Program | greenpower.gov.au |
| Smart Approved Watermark | smartwatermark.org |
| EnviroDevelopment | envirodevelopment.com.au |

| | | |
|---|---|---|
| **Water saving** | Green Plumbers | greenplumbers.com.au |
| | Savewater! Alliance | savewater.com.au |
| | Saving Water, NSW | sydneywater.com.au/SavingWater/InYourHome |
| | Water Care | watercare.sa.gov.au |
| **Green power** | Australian Government Accreditation | greenpower.gov.au |
| | ActewAGL (ACT) | actewagl.com.au |
| | AGL (National) | agl.com.au |
| | Country Energy (National) | countryenergy.com.au |
| | Energex (QLD) | energex.com.au |
| | Energy Australia (National) | energy.com.au |
| | Ergon Energy (QLD) | ergon.com.au |
| | Green Switch (National) | greenswitch.com |
| | Integral Energy (NSW/QLD) | integralenergy.com.au |
| | Jackgreen (National) | jackgreen.com.au |
| | Origin Energy (National) | originenergy.com.au |
| | True Energy (VIC) | truenergy.com.au |
| | Western Power (WA) | westernpower.com.au |
| **Procurement** | Ecospecifier | ecospecifier.org |
| | Australian Green Procurement | greenhouse.gov.au |
| | Buy Recycled WA | zerowastewa.com.au |
| | Buy Recycled Business Alliance | brba.com.au |
| **Think tanks, resources & community groups** | Natural Edge Project | naturaledgeproject.net |
| | Urban Ecology Australia | urbanecology.org.au |
| | Alternative Technology Association | ata.org.au |
| | Australian and New Zealand Solar Energy Society | anzses.org |
| | Earth Building Association of Australia EBAA | ebaa.asn.au |
| | Australian City Farms & Community Gardens Network | communitygarden.org.au |
| | Get Green Water Conservation Ideas | getgreen.com.au |
| | Natural Strategies Group | naturalstrategies.com.au |
| **Action & education groups** | Clean Up Australia | cleanup.org.au |
| | Australian Conservation Foundation | acfonline.org.au |
| | Friends of the Earth | foe.org.au |
| | Greenpeace | greenpeace.com.au |
| | Climate Positive | climatepositive.org |
| | Planet Ark | planetark.com |
| | WWF | wwf.org.au |

# websites

| | |
|---|---|
| Keep Australia Beautiful | kab.org.au |
| Landcare Australia | landcareonline.com.au |
| Nature Conservation Council of NSW | nccnsw.org.au |
| Total Environment Centre | tec.org.au |
| Greenfleet | greenfleet.com.au |
| The Environment Centre Northern Territory | ecnt.org |
| Cycling Promotion Fund | rideabike.com.au |
| Australian Rainforest Foundation | arf.net.au |
| Clean Ocean Foundation | cleanocean.org |
| Greening Australia | greeningaustralia.org.au |
| The Wilderness Society | wilderness.org.au |
| Wildlife Preservation Society of Australia | wpsa.org.au |
| Western Conservation Alliance | npansw.org.au/wca-bbs |
| Waterwatch Australia | waterwatch.org.au |
| OzGREEN | ozgreen.org.au |
| The Oceania Project | oceania.org.au |
| The Mineral Policy Institute | mpi.org.au |
| Marine Coastal Community Network | mccn.org.au/home |
| Indigenous Flora and Fauna Association | iffa.org.au |
| 60 Day Carbon Challenge | carbonchallenge.com.au |

**Green products**

| | |
|---|---|
| Todae | todae.com.au |
| Bird Textiles | birdtextile.com |
| Biome | biome.com.au |
| All Eco | alleco.com.au |
| Eco Depot | ecodepot.com.au |
| Neco | neco.com.au |
| Energy Matters | renewablestore.com.au |

**Cleaning products**

| | |
|---|---|
| Sonett | sonett-online.de/1eng/home_e |
| Laundry Ball | laundryball.com.au |
| Bee Green Building Council of Australia | beegreen.com.au |
| Clean Conscience | cleanconscience.com.au |
| Energy Health & Living | enviroqld.com.au |
| Naturally for You | naturallyforyou.com.au |
| Non-Toxic Life | nontoxiclife.com.au |
| Tri Nature | trinature.com |

**Baby products**

| | |
|---|---|
| Ecobabe | ecobabe.com.au |
| EcoEssentials | ecoessentials.com.au |

| | | |
|---|---|---|
| **Sustainable kitchens & furniture** | Sustainable Living Fabrics | greenliving.com.au/slf |
| | Circle Interiors | circleinteriors.com |
| | Going Green Solutions | goinggreensolutions.com.au |
| | Environment Shop | environmentshop.com.au |
| | Multipowered Products | multipoweredproducts.com.au |
| | EcoLinen | ecolinen.com |
| **General green shopping** | Bird Textiles | birdtextile.com |
| | E Cycled | e-cycled.com |
| | Blessed Earth | blessedearth.com.au |
| | Tontine Insulation | tontinefibres.com.au |
| | The Freecycle Network | freecycle.org |
| | Pure Pod | purepod.com.au |
| | Australian Farmers Association | farmersmarkets.org.au |
| | No Sweat Shop label | nosweatshoplabel.com |
| | Fully stoked | fullystoked.com.au |
| | Oxfam | oxfam.org.au/shop |
| | Elsom | elsom.com.au |
| | Gorman | gorman.ws/default.aspx#/gorman/organic/organic_02 |
| | Sara Victoria | saravictoria.com.au/ecofashionshow |
| | Viridis Luxe | viridisluxe.com |
| | Soap in a Nutshell | soapinanutshell.com.au |
| | BoxSmart | boxsmart.com.au |
| | The Natural Paint Place | thenaturalpaintplace.com.au |
| **State agencies** | Australian Capital Territory | environment.act.gov.au |
| | New South Wales | environment.nsw.gov.au |
| | Northern Territory | nt.gov.au/nreta |
| | Queensland | epa.qld.gov.au |
| | South Australia | environment.sa.gov.au |
| | Tasmania | dtae.tas.gov.au |
| | Victoria | dse.vic.gov.au |
| | Western Australia | environment.wa.gov.au |
| | Department of Conservation (NZ) | doc.govt.nz |
| **Directories** | Organic Food Directory | organicfooddirectory.com.au |
| | Green Product and Service Eco Directory | thegreendirectory.com.au |
| | Green Pages | thegreenpages.com.au |

# glossary

**biodegradable>** capable of decaying as a result of the action of micro-organisms that break the material down into naturally recyclable elements.

**biodiversity>** all life on earth, including the variability within it and between ecological communities or systems.

**carbon emission>** carbon substances like carbon monoxide and carbon dioxide that pollute the atmosphere and contribute to global warming.

**carbon footprint>** the impact a person or business has on the environment in terms of the amount of greenhouse gases produced, measured in units of carbon dioxide.

**carbon sequestration>** also known as carbon pooling or carbon sinking, carbon sequestration means capturing and storing carbon in forests, soils or in the oceans, so as to reduce the build-up of carbon dioxide in the atmosphere. Carbon sequestration is encouraged through enriching soils, oceans or underground geological repositories with elements that increase the uptake of carbon. Currently, increasing carbon storage in above-ground ecosystems is the most widely used, as it is the easiest and most immediate option.

**carcinogen>** a cancer-causing substance.

**climate change>** the variation in the Earth's climate over time, largely involving temperature changes in the atmosphere. Scientists believe dangerous climate change is being caused by global warming, which is in turn significantly spurred on by greenhouse gas emissions.

**compact flourescent lights (CFLs)>** a style of light bulb that significantly reduces energy usage. Derived from the flourescent tubes invented in the 1970s, CFLs emit the same amount of visible light, use less power and have a longer rated life. Some concern now exists around their safe disposal.

**companion planting>** the planting of different crops close to each other, in order to take advantage of the plants' natural properties to help the others.

**conservation>** sustainable use and protection of natural resources including plants, animals, mineral deposits, soils, clean water, clean air, and fossil fuels such as coal, petroleum and natural gas.

**dioxin>** the popular name for a family of organic compounds that bio-accumulate with toxic effect in humans and wildlife. Two of the most widely studied sources of dioxins are the making of the herbicide Agent Orange and the chlorine bleaching of wood pulp in paper-making.

**double glazing>** window treatment in which air is trapped between two panes of glass, creating an insulating barrier that reduces heat loss, noise and condensation. While double glazing is only slowly coming into popularity in Australia, Europeans are now using triple-glazed windows.

**ecological footprint>** the amount of biologically productive land and sea area needed to generate the resources a human population consumes, and to absorb the corresponding waste.

**ecosystem>** the interaction of plants, animals and the environment.

**embodied energy>** the production of a building or product requires a certain amount of energy, ranging from the mining and manufacturing of raw materials to transporting them and even the administrative processes involved in producing it; also, maintenance or renovation can add further embodied energy. An assessment for embodied energy takes into consideration all those processes.

**energy star rating>** a mandatory government labelling system for some (not all) electronic appliances: the higher the number of stars, the more efficient the appliance.

**e-waste>** discarded electrical equipment such as mobile phones, computers, DVD players and cabling.

**Fairtrade>** a certification system that labels products that meet 'fair' environmental, ethical labour and developmental standards.

**food miles>** the distance food travels from the source of its growth to the consumer's table.

**formaldehyde>** a chemical often used in disinfectant because of its bacteria-killing properties, but which has also been classified as a carcinogen.

**genetic engineering>** directly manipulating the genes (DNA) of an organism in order to change its character. Concerns about genetic engineering include disruption of natural ecosystems and the unknown long-term effects of genetically modified crop consumption.

**global warming>** the accelerated warming of the Earth's surface due to release of greenhouse gases generated from industrial activity and deforestation. The possible results of global warming include rising sea levels, increasing intensity of extreme weather events, changes in amount and pattern of rain and snow, changes in crop yields and ocean trade routes, glacier retreat, species extinctions and increases in disease

**green electricity>** electricity obtained from renewable sources, such as wind, sun and water, not fossil fuels such as coal or oil.

**greenhouse effect>** the Earth's atmosphere allows solar radiation to be absorbed by the planet's surface, which is then re-emitted as heat. This heat is in turn reflected back by gases such as carbon dioxide, methane, nitrous oxide and ozone that are in the atmosphere (greenhouse gases). This is the greenhouse effect that keeps the earth warm. The increasing release of greenhouse gases into the atmosphere is causing global warming.

**greenhouse gases>** gases such as methane and carbon dioxide ($CO_2$) that contribute to the greenhouse effect.

**greenpower>** Australian Government system that denotes power sourced from the sun, wind, water and waste, and sold by electricity companies.

**grey water>** grey water is fresh drinking water that has been used for cleaning in the kitchen, laundry or bathroom (not the toilet). It comprises 50–80 per cent of residential waste water.

**heat gain>** the heat accumulated in a building through different sources such as outdoor temperature and humidity levels, but also people inside it, lights, computer, copiers, fridges and ovens. Most of the heat is usually gained through the sun beating down on the roof and pouring through windows.

**indoor air quality>** the purity of the air in an enclosed space. There are many sources of pollution in any indoor space, much of it deriving from building materials and furniture treatments, but also from insulation, cleaning products, pesticides, paints and even outdoor pollution. Inadequate ventilation, heat and humidity levels can also contribute to indoor pollution.

# glossary

**insulation>** insulation consists of material applied to ceilings, walls, floors and the roof to reduce the rate of heat transfer through the external surfaces of a building – like wrapping a blanket around a house. Insulation can consist of natural or synthetic materials, or a combination of both. Experts distinguish between two types of insulation: bulk and reflective. Bulk insulation, as the name implies, adds extra mass to the walls to stop heat transfer, while the second type of insulation literally reflects the heat.

**kWh>** a kilowatt hour is a unit of energy measuring 1000 watt hours; the amount of energy produced or transferred in one hour by one kilowatt of power.

**landfill>** a site where waste is placed in the ground. This can happen in a controlled or uncontrolled way, and usually refers to waste that cannot be recycled but is left to decompose.

**LED>** this stands for light emitting diode. LEDs are semi-conductor diodes that typically emit a single wavelength of light when charged with electricity. First introduced in the 1970s, LEDs use less energy than simple incandescent light globes, are virtually indestructible and last for decades.

**life cycle analysis (LCA)>** all building products can affect the environment in many ways during every stage of their life, whether this is in production or after it's been discarded. A life cycle analysis looks at all these stages 'from cradle to grave', beginning with the acquisition of raw materials, manufacturing and shipping processes, and its effects throughout its use (such as indoor air quality, durability and performance), as well as how easy it is to recycle or reuse the material at the end of its life.

**methane>** a gas emitted by organic matter breaking down.

**old-growth forest>** an ancient and unique area of forest that cannot be replicated and has not been destroyed by logging. They often contain rare fauna and flora species, and store large amounts of greenhouse gases.

**operational energy>** the energy that is used to operate a particular device or accumulation of devices. The energy used by all the appliances, light sources and heating in a home amounts to the operational energy of that building.

**organic>** produced without fossil fuel-based fertilisers, synthetic pesticides or genetically modified crop varieties.

**orientation>** refers to the way a new building is positioned on a site in relation to cardinal points and the sun. The first principle for building a sustainable home is ideal orientation so as to maximise the benefits derived from sunlight and passive heating, as well as prevalent wind directions and shade. Good orientation makes a building more comfortable to live in and cheaper to run.

**ozone layer>** the layer in the Earth's atmosphere that absorbs harmful ultraviolet radiation from the sun. A depleting ozone layer allows more radiation to pass through, causing genetic damage to life on Earth. Ozone levels are depleted by the release of gases like chlorofluorocarbons (CFCs) contained in products such as CFC aerosol sprays, now banned in most countries.

**passive design>** passive design is design that does not require mechanical heating or cooling, instead drawing advantage from a home's orientation and spatial configuration. Homes that are passively designed take advantage of natural energy flows to maintain thermal comfort.

**passive solar technologies>** technologies that convert sunlight into usable heat for water or air, cause air movement for ventilating, or store heat for future use without the assistance of other energy sources. They do so without active mechanical systems, as opposed to active solar systems, which use pumps or fans to increase usable heat in a system.

**photovoltaic power>** photovoltaic panels, installed on roofs or near homes, generate electricity using the sun's light, unlike the solar panels used for heating water, which absorb heat. A panel consists of multiple cells made up of semi-conducting silicon and when this is exposed to light, electrical charges are generated that can be conducted away by metal contacts as direct current.

**permaculture>** a garden or farming system that uses a variety of plants to encourage self-sufficient crop production.

**product miles>** the amount of energy needed to get a product to the customer. The term is used as a measurement of the environmental impact of bringing any product to market.

**renewable resource>** a renewable resource is one that can be replaced over time by natural processes, such as fish populations or natural vegetation, or is inexhaustible, such as solar energy.

**sick building syndrome>** a term used to describe physical discomfort felt by building occupants, often with severe implications on their health, that can be attributed to the building, its structure or furnishings. Often, sick building syndrome is related to indoor air quality.

**self-sufficient>** able to provide for one's own needs without external intervention or assistance.

**solar power>** system of collecting solar energy (from the sun) to generate electricity; power created by converting sunlight into electricity.

**sustainable>** a sustainable process or state is one that can be maintained in its original form indefinitely. That is, a system that will not collapse or break down. For example, creating energy from fossil fuels that will eventually run out is not a sustainable practice.

**sustainable product development (SPD)>** a method of product development that improves efficiency and lowers environmental impact by reducing the impact of raw materials, processing and waste.

**thermal mass>** generally, any material that has the capacity to store heat. When applied correctly, thermal mass can significantly reduce the requirement for active heating and cooling systems and the consumption of active solar, renewable energy and especially fossil fuel technologies.

**volatile organic compounds (VOCs)>** these are the fumes that evaporate from conventional pesticides, cleaning products, paints, finishes and glues. Harmful to animal and plant life, they can also jeopardise human health and make a significant contribution to indoor air quality. VOCs are held responsible for causing sick building syndrome.

**WELS (Water Efficiency Labelling and Standards)>** the Australian Government system for labelling the efficiency of water-using products such as showerheads. The more stars, the more efficient the product. The label also shows the product's water consumption in litres per minute.

## about Clean Up Australia

Solo around-the-world yachtsman Ian Kiernan couldn't believe the amount of rubbish he saw floating in the world's oceans during his epic voyage in 1986–87, and decided to do something about it.

In 1989, with Kim McKay and a group of close friends, he formed Clean Up Australia. Clean Up Australia Day is held on the first Sunday in March each year when hundreds of thousands of volunteers gather at more than 7500 sites across the nation to remove rubbish from our parks, waterways, beaches and roadsides.

All year round, Clean Up Australia is committed to cleaning up our climate and is involved in school and community environmental education and action campaigns.

This Australian initiative has been exported through the Clean Up the World campaign run in conjunction with the United Nations Environment Program (UNEP). Each September, millions of volunteers in over 120 countries are now involved.

You can help either as a volunteer by giving your time, or by joining Clean Up Australia and making a regular contribution. All donations are tax deductable.

Support Clean Up at **www.cleanup.org.au** or call **1800 282 329**.

> *'We can all make a difference and joining Clean Up is a simple and practical way to do something about climate change. Be part of it, start today to save tomorrow and help Clean Up Our Climate!'*
>
> Ian Kiernan, AO, 1994 Australian of the Year, chairman and founder, Clean Up Australia and Clean Up the World

## acknowledgements

**Kim McKay**, AO (right) is co-founder and deputy chairwoman of Clean Up Australia and Clean Up the World. An international social and sustainability marketing consultant, Kim counts *National Geographic* among her many clients. In 2008 she was made an Officer of the Order of Australia for distinguished service to the environment and the community.

**Jenny Bonnin** (left) is a director of Clean Up Australia and Clean Up the World. She and Kim founded Momentum2, a social and sustainability marketing firm, and together created the True Green brand. Jenny has recently embarked on a role with the Clinton Climate Initiative in Sydney to further her passion for creating a sustainable future. She has two children and two stepchildren.

Kim and Jenny's previous books – *True Green: 100 everyday ways you can contribute to a healthier planet* (ABC Books, 2006); *True Green @ Work: 100 ways you can make the environment your business* with business writer Tim Wallace (ABC Books, 2007); and *True Green Kids: 100 things you can do to save the planet* (ABC Books, 2008) have also been published in the United States by National Geographic Books.

**Marian Kyte** is a freelance designer and creative director of True Green. She has a passion for incorporating sustainability principles into her work. Her clients have included Qantas, Craftsman House Books, Power Publications, Sherman Galleries, *Art & Australia*, *Limelight* magazine and True Green. Her son Locky is her inspiration.

**Vivanne Stappmans** is a researcher and writer with degrees in journalism and design, and has spent years writing about places, people and homes. Well versed and ever curious about design, Vivanne has explored, interviewed, written and edited for many of Australia's leading publications.

*True Green Home* has helped consolidate our True Green family of colleagues and supporters. We could not hope to do a True Green book without Marian Kyte who is an endless source of creative inspiration and joy. It never ceases to amaze us how she can illustrate our points in the most colourful, simple and brilliant ways.

Vivanne Stappmans managed to deliver the research and a beautiful baby girl, Ivy, at the same time! She's an incredibly clever and generous writer who cares deeply about her daughter's future. Thanks also to Helen Littleton for her clever, insightful editing and the splendid Brigitta Doyle, managing editor at ABC Books, who believes in us and supports us in so many ways. ABC Books' publicist, Jane Finemore, continues to provide valued and smart guidance.

We especially want to thank our erstwhile marketing coordinator, Kylie Guthrie, who has kept her eye on the ball though the book's planning and production and who is a rock in our office. We also thank all the experts who contributed their insights for the feature pages of the book and salute the green architects and designers of Australia for helping to transform the way we live. Special thanks to our fellow Clean Up directors and the Clean Up staff for their continued support.

We dedicate this book to the favourite builder in our lives, Ian Kiernan, who loves nothing more than brandishing his tape measure on a building site and creating beautiful restored buildings from virtual rubble. He is a true builder in so many ways, and his dedication to building a better future for the Australian and global environment through Clean Up and countless green technology projects must never be forgotten.

'Our personal consumer choices have ecological, social, and spiritual consequences. It is time to re-examine some of our deeply held notions that underlie our lifestyles'

**David Suzuki**, award-winning scientist, environmentalist and broadcaster

Elysium House 7 by Andrew Maynard Architects. Rendering: Virtuocity